D EDICATION

Henley and Dakota

You bring joy, magic, and giggles to every aspect of our lives. I thought being a parent was the absolute best feeling until I met each of you.

I have been in love with you, long before you were born.

Acknowledgement

I have changed a few names of individuals in order to preserve their anonymity, as well as part of the timeline because it took me over 20 years to pull this story together. Although these are my memories of the facts of our lives, when required, I relied on my mom to fill in the gaps from when we were very young.

A very special thank you to my friend Erin Morrisey Martinez for taking a writing journey with me. Without your profound intelligence, love of reading and "mad" editing skills, this book may not have found its way here.

Thank you to my wonderful - all grown up children, for your unconditional love, humor, and sarcasm. Especially the sarcasm; without it, humor would have been scarce along the way, and the journey would have been so much harder. The day each of you were born can be described as two of the most beautiful days of my life. Your births were each so different and I lovingly remember every detail!

Mom, I am grateful for learning many things from you. How you survived so much at a young age blows me away. If I had to name just one thing that I am grateful for, I guess it would be the importance of laughing and dancing.

Thank you for loving us Uncle Gary and helping Mom when we were young!

A very special thank you to my husband. At times, I know you felt like I could not hear you howling in sheer agony to get my attention, but I did listen to you! I am grateful you stayed engaged in our lives and encouraged me to finish this book. Thank you for your twisted sense of humor!

Jaimers - aka Meaghan, although this is a love story about your mom, I would be remiss if I said it is not a love story to you as well -- to your life. **You are your mother's daughter and that is a beautiful thing!** I know your mom would be proud of you because I am. She continues to live within us, laughing! Geez, her laugh was crazy awesome. She would be shocked about all that has happened during her time away. Thank you too, Dave for loving her as we do.

Brie, I've learned about setting boundaries from you. Not an easy lesson for me! I hate limitations; everyone knows that about me. I prefer to be smack dab in the middle of your life. It's a selfish desire to be close to the one's I love. I am learning I cannot have that position. I respect that as I appreciate and love you.

Denise, you are not just my sister in law; I consider you my sister. Thank you for your guidance along the way and the encouragement to edit, edit, edit. **Especially thank you for your final help with editing. There is no way this book would be as polished without your work on it!** Also, thank you for always showing me the humor in my life.

To my sisters by "choice" - Carolyn Hallett, Carla Ten Broeck, and Cabrini Sanchez. "You are not the boss of me."

To my gorgeous cousin, Didi. Okay, what can I say about my feelings for you? Although we missed out on growing up closer, I feel blessed that we found each other – even later in life! You once looked at me and said: "I cannot believe the things you went through while raising Caleb alone." That made me rethink my life, and for the first time, I saw it through someone else's eyes. Thank you for pointing me in the right direction and for sending me cheerful, raunchy cards along the way!

Don, I love and adore you and have many great memories of us as we were growing up. I especially love bantering with you over the fact that I messed up your face while pumping you on my death trap bike, and that you got a filthy fishhook stuck to my eyelid when we were young. All accidentally, of course!

Jason, the day you were born was a day I have never forgotten. We slicked you up with baby oil and played with you for hours. I am proud of the dad you have become as well as the fact that you were able to start your own business doing what you love.

Juli Bradley Wretschko and Kellie Odom Robison, you are my oldest friends. I have many beautiful and fun memories of us as kids and teens. Thank you for your unconditional love.

To all the many men and women that helped teach me about life – I thank you from the bottom of my heart. To all my cousins – the ones I am close to and the ones from afar, I love you...each of you.

T HANK YOU FOR READING MY BOOK!

THE DAISY
My sister's favorite flower.

Daisies symbolize innocence and purity.
According to legend, whenever an infant died, God
sprinkled daisies over the earth to cheer the parents up.

A daisy also symbolizes new beginnings. I
am all about new beginnings. Do-overs.

Start-ups. Taking first steps. Making fresh starts.
Burying the hatchet. Turning over a new leaf.

Forgiving and forgetting.

Carry on - one day at a time.

LIFE BEYOND THE KITCHEN DOOR
By
Denine Turner

CONTENTS

T HE BEGINNING

My story begins on a hot and muggy day in Albuquerque. Location: our little kitchen in the North Valley. No breeze, just hot and unusually humid. The swamp cooler takes on a life of its own, spewing out a musty, God-awful odor. I told Carlos not to turn it off yesterday, but did he listen? No! So, on top of everything else, we are urgently trying to get done, we must work with that damned smell. It should be all hands-on deck, as we are catering a significant outdoor sit-down wedding for 200 guests. To summarize - all food, flowers, wedding and groom cake, tables, chairs, full bar, linens, dishware. You name it; we have been hired to handle every detail.

We are dragging butt today. We are exhausted from back-to-back daily events all month in the sweltering heat. It is sad how *life* can happen in unexpected ways, and not always as we would like. No order, no warning, just calamity.

Someone yells out for me to get the phone, "Denine, you have a call."

I ask who it is.

"Some lady."

"Take a message, please."

"No, she said you *have* to come to the phone."

"Great, just what I need right now. It better be an emergency – 'Hello, can I help you?'"

"Denine?"

"Deb, is that you? Where are you? I thought Mom said you would be here by now?"

"I am in the bath," my sister says.

"When will you be here, Deb? Really, I must go. Why are you calling me? Do you plan on coming to the kitchen today? Is something wrong – and *why* are you calling from the tub – that's weird?"

"I found a lump."

"Where?"

"On my left breast."

"Oh, great... do you want me to come over?"

Before she even answers me, I am praying she says no. We have no time for family drama today.

"No, don't come, I will be leaving soon, but I wanted you to know first."

"Why first, it doesn't mean you have cancer. How big is it?" She replies, "It feels small."

"Then, get your ass here. You will be fine. Deb, I will go with you later to get it checked out, but we can't do that until we get through this weekend from hell."

"Okay, I will see you soon. Do you want me to stop for anything before I get there?"

"Yes, could you run by the winery to check on the rental order? There should be some boys there setting up; make sure they are *really* working and not messing around. See if the set-up is correct. I left a template taped to the wall by the warmers."

For a moment, a tiny moment, I thought I should tell Mom about my conversation with Deb. Nope, screw that! We will deal with it next week. My sister is an alcoholic and has never been in the best health. She is the person that everyone loves -- open-minded — our family hippie. Over the years, she and I battle different issues, sometimes even over a game of Monopoly. She would win, but I would die trying to beat her.

One thing is certain; we are close. We know what the other is thinking even before one of us utters a word. When Caleb and Meaghan were little, Deb and I did everything together. Our fun day was going to the laundromat. We would load up 27 loads of laundry (between us), stuff the kids anywhere they would fit, and off we went.

Piling out of the car was an event in and of itself. It was like a game for the kids. We would laugh at ourselves, sometimes close to peeing our pants! The kids always had fun, and it never felt like a chore.

We learned to love dancing from watching our mom. We would dance at home, crank up the stereo as loud as possible, and lose ourselves. The kids would join in sometimes, but even if they didn't, we would still dance. We didn't care how stupid we looked. To this day, I absentmindedly still crank it up when I am doing chores, or in my car, it doesn't matter. Mom taught us to do the *shimmy*. It's all about the boobs.

Over the years, Deb has been her own worst enemy. She does not intend to get drunk, but as soon as she starts to drink, the result is always the same. After the kids leave for school, Deb opens a beer to clean the house. Before long, she has consumed an entire six-pack, and it's not even noon. She has struggled with it, and we struggle with her.

Occasionally, she stops drinking and is good for a while. Once she was sober for almost two years, but that was because I had her committed on a three-day hold after I found her near-death from alcohol poisoning. The judge ordered her to stay in the facility for at least a month. She stayed for three and didn't speak to me for the entire duration. I would visit her, but she denied my visits and when she was released, it took her a while to contact me. Eventually our lives resumed and we never discussed it again.

She is a great mom during her sobriety. And, I mean, great. Much better than I ever am as a sober mom! When Bailey was born, she and Deb became thick as thieves. Instantly in love with one another. They have always been very close. While growing up, Deb could be rebellious, but at the same time, she was the first one to stop and help if someone needed it. At any cost to herself, she would give you the shirt off her own back: stray people, stray dogs, and cats. If someone needed help and they crossed her path, you could count on the fact that she would do just about anything to help.

How did we get here? Why are we faced with another crisis? This family has never had a break. Life as we know it has never been the same since we left California, almost 35 years ago.

CHAPTER 1 - HITCHING A RIDE

I've often wondered how Mom survived so many tragedies when we were little. They seemed to come quickly, one right after the other. In writing this story, I relied on my memories, but to recall them, I had to permit myself to look back at how the story began and at times, relive that pain. The oldest of five children, my mom, learned at an early age to be strong. It was her strength that saved us. As the story goes, my biological father worked for the USDA Forestry Department in California for about 18 months before officially quitting.

We lived near the beach, which is probably why I still have a desire to live near the water. After living through the Watts Riots, Mom knew we needed more stability, so only a month after the riots ended, we were able to move into an apartment. She jumped at the chance to have a better roof over our heads. Even if it was small, it was far from the dangerous Watts neighborhood.

Mom told us that she hit the wall with my father. In her words, she said, "I had had enough." After months of my father being out of work, she decided to leave him. It was his choice not to work. He was not laid off. He did not want to work. His laziness outraged her, and she grew to hate him. Mom could not understand why the love of her life and father to her three young children would choose not to work when so many people were desperate to find a job back then.

She was more than willing to clean houses or take in ironing. However, the people she knew did not have money for such indulgences. She had three small kids to take care of, which made it harder for her to find work outside the little apartment we lived in, and *he* could not be trusted to watch us.

My sister Deb was the oldest at five, I was almost four, and Matt was a baby. Mom was never afraid of leaving our father; she only had reservations about how she would feed us once she walked out that door. Our grandparents would let us move in with them, but no one had money to help. Not even for bus fares. Even worse, we did not have any family in California, and she knew the only way we would survive would be to get back to New Mexico. She had no choice.

The plan was in motion. While he went out, we left. We only took the clothes that we were wearing, and nine peanut butter and jelly sandwiches *(crust on)* cut in half on the diagonal and stuffed back into the bread wrapper.

In October of 1965, with Matt in her arms, Deb and I walked behind our mother, holding hands, and staying right at her heels. If we lagged at all, Mom could feel us slipping away so she would stop, turn around, and scold us to keep up. That was how it went as we walked down the busy road, headed to the interstate. Hitchhiking today would be very dangerous, but back then, it was standard. It may not have been that normal for a woman with three kids, but there was no other choice at the time. She had a plan and was hopeful we would get rides now and then, and we could walk in between the rides. We had no money, and the sandwiches would not last long if we didn't get a ride.

In Mom's desperation to save us, she had not considered other options. Her inner strength was her guide; she knew we would make it because failure was not an option. Matt was still on a bottle, which meant he would starve if he didn't have milk. Mom packed bottles but did not have a plan for preventing the milk from spoiling.

The bottles did get warm, and she was afraid to let Matt drink them. The last thing she needed was a sick baby on her hands. According to her, by the time we got to the interstate, my sister and I had to pee again. Luckily, there was a truck stop with a restroom, restaurant, and souvenir/convenience store. Mom left Deb and me alone in the restroom, and after a few minutes, she and Matt returned with refrigerator-cold milk.

I have heard this story most of my life, but the real miracle exemplified on that day was the fact that Mom was only 22 ½ years old. At that tender age, she had more love and determination than most older people. She could have given us all away, but she chose to keep us. To love and raise us.

Years later, she told us she stole the milk, and luckily for us, a friendly family driving to Texas offered to drive us all the way to New Mexico. I believe Mom when she says leaving California was one of the easiest yet hardest thing she ever did.

The foundation was set for the next phase of a long and challenging life.

No regrets here! My DNA has always had a story to tell. Fundamentally, my good and bad characteristics are unchangeable. Even if I could have skipped the heartaches, I would be exactly who I am today. Never do I feel like I have the right to expect more out of my life, yet I am grateful for all I have been given. Intentionally I embrace all aspects of my life: the good, the bad – and the *real* ugly parts. I have learned to roll with the punches, and there have been a lot! When my kids were born, I knew I would feel their pain, sorrows, and triumphs- in big ways! They would be the gravity to keep me on this earth!

Over the years, Mom taught me to cook, and I am pretty good when I want or need to be, but this doesn't include the tuna casserole my kids grew up on and hate to this day.

I have a funny memory of when my younger brothers were in elementary school. I was sitting on a barstool in the kitchen as Mom started to make their lunches. My brother Jason was also in the kitchen, watching Mom, sleepily. She moved around the kitchen, retrieving items from the cabinets and the fridge. She plopped down all the stuff directly onto the beautiful, hand-painted tile countertop and began assembling the sandwiches first.

She started by spreading softened unsalted butter onto

each piece of crustless bread. Four pieces, to be exact. A sandwich for each kid. And yes, it was crustless! She continued making the sandwiches by wrapping and folding over each piece of thinly sliced roasted turkey onto two slices of bread. To me, it looked like ribbon candy.

Holy cow! Then came the cheese and lettuce. Finally, she smeared a small dollop of real mayo (not Miracle Whip) onto the lettuce, just before topping it with the other piece of bread. It was only 7:00 a.m., and Jason and I were at full attention, watching her in amazement. She was still not done. Jesus Christ, she was *still* not done!

She sliced on the diagonal right before piercing each half with matching "frilly" toothpicks and then carefully crammed them into small plastic sandwich bags. The toothpicks poked through, but I am confident that error would go unnoticed. As we watched our mother make that masterpiece of a simple sandwich, I knew I would never forget that morning.

Afterward, the only words spoken came out of Jason's mouth: "Mom, I am going to get beaten up today if anyone sees that sandwich."

We often laugh about this story because we have a need to laugh at everything. Sad stuff, bad stuff, and even death can be humorous. Our laughter has caused many misunderstandings over the years with others, but it helps us survive.

To say Mom has a love for food is an understatement, and probably one of the reasons she started her catering business. To this day, she has piles of cookbooks that she knows intimately. If you ask her about a recipe, Mom knows precisely where it is and how to tweak it just so. Over the years, she developed many original recipes. She even created a cake recipe we are renowned for in Albuquerque. We receive calls about it all the time, along the lines of, "Are you the company with *that* cake?" We have made lifetime customers and friends because of it.

I have an accounting degree, so I have embraced all aspects of the business, from soup to nuts. I can plan, budget, shop, prepare, and serve an event, then do payroll on Monday. When you have a small, family-owned-and-operated business, you wear many hats. Mom and I each bring our talents to the company, which allows us to complement and not compete with one another. I am agreeable because it is not my business.

We have had the privilege to cater weddings, bar and bat mitzvahs, funerals, graduations, baby, and wedding showers. I am proud to say; we catered an event that President George W. Bush attended before he became President. Gracious and humble are the descriptors that come to mind when we think of him.

Many years later, while catering an event in Albuquerque in 2007, my then eight-year-old nephew who begged to go and promised to stay in the back area with the staff, received a gift he still treasures—a presidential American flag lapel pin. President George W. Bush, our 43rd president, took it off his jacket and pinned it directly onto his shirt. From the viewpoint of those in the "back of the house," we will never forget President Bush's kind demeanor, which we experienced first-hand. Suffice it to say; we have created and observed many events that taught us great life lessons.

Today, Deb often works, or as we call it, *volunteers* at the kitchen. She does not have the drive that Mom and I have—we call it our 'sickness.' However, what she brings to the table is a love of family, which grounds us. Well, occasionally, it does anyway, and whenever Deb has had enough, she leaves the kitchen. And that is that.

C HAPTER 2 – CROSSROADS

I should not be here. In February of 1962, and only a few hours after my birth, a nurse brought a different baby back to my mom. She recalled the baby was fair-skinned and had reddish hair. She knew it was not me. Mom told me she had only seen me for a moment after I was born, but it was enough to know this was not the same baby she had held earlier.

She threw a fit, explaining that her baby had dark skin and dark curly hair. After crying and some negotiating, we were given back to our rightful parents. This one itty-bitty mistake of being switched at birth could have changed the outcome of everything in my life. To this day, Mom still remembers the other family's last name. It was Eaves.

The period of August 11-16, 1965 was another pivotal time in my young life. My parents were staying in a motel in Southern California, near where the Watts Riots began. A violent act of rebellion due to the social and economic injustices in the Watts neighborhood in South Central Los Angeles. There had been tensions between the African American neighborhood and the authorities for quite some time. The riots began after a white highway patrol officer stopped a black man for reckless driving. As we know from our history books, it was the costliest urban rebellion of the Civil Rights Era.

For several days, rioters overturned and burned cars and looted and damaged grocery stores, liquor stores, and department stores. In the end, nothing changed, other than $40 million in property damage, thousands injured, and several deaths - a direct result from the riots.

Mom's first thought turned to her three kids. She was afraid. Worried, we could be hurt. Near the motel was a swimming pool located at the back of the property, which was furthest from the fighting. Mom thought it was the safest place for Deb and me. I know if Mom thought we would be more out of harm's way in the pool, that was where she would put us.

According to her memory, she put us in the pool, and we hunkered down near the shallow end for several hours. You could hear the looting and shots firing in the background. Matt was placed in the bathtub and slept there for several hours while our dad dozed off and on while watching TV. When the gunfire and looting stopped, Mom wanted to celebrate the end of the riots by having a picnic by the pool. We kids' loved the water, and it was better than staying cooped up in the motel room.

As if sleeping mere feet from the violence was not enough danger to experience and live through, our family endured another freakish nightmare. Although I was very young, I vividly recall the pain of being yanked by my arm as I was launched from the bottom of the deep end of the pool to the surface of the water. With her kind eyes and boobs popping out of the top of her bathing suit, Mom frantically leaned over to pull me out of the pool.

The squishy sound the water made as it poured off Dad's wet jeans and cowboy boots that he was wearing before he dove in and saved me, is the cause of my déjà-vu moments! Today, whenever I hear that sound, it almost always gives me goosebumps.

For most of my life, this was a suppressed memory – forgotten until recently. More than likely had another minute passed before I was pulled out, I would have been included in the statistics of children drowning while parents sat nearby not supervising correctly. I am confident this was the kindest gesture this man would ever do for me.

The universe would demand I learn hard lessons; living a simple life as a good person would never be enough. Decades would pass before I could figure out "the how and the why" we had to go through so much tragedy.

In July of 1969, our family dealt with yet another big tragedy. While driving to Questa, New Mexico, with our grandfather, we were in a horrific car accident. Freakish summertime snowstorms are frequent in New Mexico, especially in the northern area. Questa is near Taos, New Mexico. After the screeching of the metal from the impact stopped, horrified, I remember my poor sister sitting right next to me on the seat - attached to the door of the old car. The door was literally inside her body. Grandpa's car must have been a Buick or some other large boat type. Blood was everywhere.

Seconds before the accident, Matt was asleep in the area above the back seat near the large window. Ejected from the car at impact, Matt and Mom were both lying on opposite sides of the road. It was surreal. The snow mixed with the blood reminded me of the cherry snow cones we had eaten just days before our trip. The accident was awful, and I had no idea if my family would live or die. Blood was pouring from mom's face as well as Matt's head. My grandpa's head was bleeding, too. My leg was barely fractured.

Deb and I not being ejected from the car was *my* punishment to watch her as she appeared to bleed to death right before my eyes.

A beautiful, tiny Asian woman with very long, black hair appeared. At first, she was not sure who to help. I believe she was the wife of the semi-truck driver that my grandpa hit. All our injuries were minor in comparison with Deb's. The door was smashed in, and the force of the accident shoved Deb into it. She was fighting for her life.

After a couple of months, although still recovering from her injuries, we knew she would be okay. She lost her spleen that day, which became the source of poor health most of her life. It should have been *me* that lost my spleen. Only moments before impact, I had fought with her. I begged to switch places with her because the scenery on the other side of the car was better. I wanted my way, and she obliged. She switched with me because Deb does not have a selfish bone in her body.

Shortly after the accident, we relocated to Roswell, New Mexico. When we were little, my mom worked as a bookkeeper by day and, to make ends meet, she worked as a bartender a few nights a week. My dad never paid one dime in child support, and Mom always worked her butt off.

At times, we would go with my grandma to receive the free food the government would hand out. I remember the cans had no labels. It was always a surprise -- you never knew what you would be eating until the can was opened. On the other side of the space, you could also get free shoes and clothing. We were always excited and grateful about getting new stuff. No matter what the free food was, Mom turned it into a nice meal.

Mom has always been what I call a clean freak, so when she returned from work at midnight, she would clean our small apartment. One night while she was cleaning, she heard a sound coming from our bedroom. My sister and I shared a bedroom, and I was almost eight years old. Instinctively, Mom grabbed the rifle that hung on the wall in our living room before going to investigate the strange noise.

As she opened our bedroom door, she saw a man's arms pulling me up through the window above our bed. I was almost to the top of the bottom part of the window, so it would not have taken much to pull me through.

She cocked the rifle and demanded he let go of me in a trembling voice. The creep paused and stared Mom down as if to say, "I am keeping her, and there is not a damned thing you can do about it." No doubt, he considered the consequences of not releasing the hold he had on me. For a split second, Mom thought I would be taken, never to be seen again. My sister, sound asleep right next to me, woke up startled. The creep dropped me, and Mom heard him scurry away into the dark; she rearranged our furniture so that our bed was no longer under a window—that very night! She also placed a wooden pole in the track of the window so it would not open and put duct tape all around the inside edge.

She told us never to open that window or remove the pole and tape. And we never did! *Almost* getting kidnapped did not only affect me. My sister was equally freaked out. From that day forward, we slept together. She was determined to keep us safe, and whenever mom was not around, she did just that!

The following morning as we were waking up, I remember the burning smell from the bleach. In mom's frustration, she must have scrubbed every corner of the apartment—her way of coping with the terror from the night before. Over the years, I rarely witnessed Mom cry. I cannot imagine how she kept it all together. She was very young, but instinctively she did what she had to for us all to survive.

Then when I was nine, I experienced another horrific pain. This time it was at the hands of the man that had saved me from drowning. I have no idea how we ended up with my father, but Matt and I were staying with him and his new wife for a brief time. He would routinely get angry and have little patience for those around him—the source of his anger!

As I lay face down on the flawlessly made bed, the stings to the back of my legs sent me to a dark place. Even as a little kid, I was pissed; that day, I learned about anger. The buckle attached to his worn-out leather belt caused welts that would leave scars I would bury deep in my soul. When the asshole was done whipping me, I was instructed to get up and go outside to play with the other children.

As I walked out of the cold room, I glanced over to see what he did next. Casually, as if he was getting dressed for the first time that day, he slid his belt back into the loops on his jeans and turned to admire himself in the mirror. As I walked down the hallway to the bathroom, I noticed blood dripping down my leg. Traumatized, I silently washed it off with toilet paper while I sat down to pee. I missed my mom.

The following morning, he proudly announced we were going out to eat breakfast—our reward for being good kids. The hard surface of the booth we were sitting in hurt my legs, and I knew I could not show pain or, even worse, cry. No doubt, my guardian angel was orchestrating the events that followed. For some reason, the man and woman that had taken us to the restaurant—my dad and his wife—each had to go to the restroom at the *exact* same time.

The minute they left the booth and walked to the back of the building, I grabbed Matt's hand, and we walked out the front door. Leaving should have scared me more, but it didn't. I believe I must have known then that I was better equipped to take care of us than he would ever be. He never liked me, and it seemed like he picked on me more than anyone else. I don't think he was always an angry, hateful person because Mom would not have been with someone like that. Maybe he didn't agree with the lessons the universe was teaching him. Who knows? To my knowledge, he never searched for us either.

Matt and I were little kids, and I had no direction or idea where I was taking us, but in desperation, I knew there was no choice but to run away. In hindsight, that remarkable day in our life was no doubt like my mom's desperation when she left our dad and hitchhiked with us from California. A police officer stopped to talk with us and offered to take us to find our mom. I later learned the officer was shocked to find two little children walking alone on a busy road.

Matt and I ended up in the same foster home for a couple of months. The foster woman's name was Rhonda, and she was very kind. As little kids, we had little information to share, so it took a couple of months for the people to understand how to contact my mom. The day she came for us, I remember feeling our lives would finally be ordinary again and safe. From that moment on, I knew I would never have a relationship with my biological father.

I also knew the only reason there was goodness in our life was because of our mother. Although the reality of not having a real dad would be the foundation of problems for my brother and sister, I would embrace it. I found it peaceful. I would not have to live in fear. Life in the '60s was not easy. Unintentionally, I learned firsthand how human character flaws can change your life. Much like our lives today, one traffic stop altered the course of history for thousands of lives, as well as our country.

I have learned to be loyal to my mom, but I have never strived to be like her. My words are reckless while hers are more kind. I am an imperfect woman with impetuous willpower. It has been the root of much pain in my life. I see that now.

During my adult years, I have experienced other weird and scary things that make me feel like my guardian angel is always with me because I am not a lucky person. You might even say I am an <u>unlucky</u> person, still trying to find my place in the world.

Who am I kidding? The truth is, I am still trying to find my place in my family, and I know it will come at a high cost.

As a young kid, I never thought much about what I wanted to be when I grew up. Money didn't seem to matter to me, and I felt like "life" would just happen for me. I found myself at a crossroads when I was about 17.

It seemed to me I would have a comfortable life if I could be an attorney or dentist. To get to that point, I needed to not only finish high school but then go to college and beyond. I didn't like school and did not get any support from my parents to take that path. There was too much conflict from family dynamics. Religion, for one thing, was one source of this conflict. We went to church — a lot. My parents followed the Church's guidance about furthering our education. They opposed it.

Then at 20 and after floundering for years, I found myself unwed and pregnant. Although I was attending a local business school, any thoughts of a real career went out the window. I didn't know it at the time, but I would live a life of more failures than successes. The harsh reality of being broke would become second nature.

Don't get me wrong, I was never close to being homeless or anything that dangerous, but life would prove to be challenging in ways that would leave deep wounds.

My name is Denine Turner. I was born in a tiny town in northern New Mexico, but I grew up in Roswell and Albuquerque, New Mexico. Roswell is an easy drive just 190 miles from Albuquerque, but I have not been back for well over 26 years. When I think of Roswell, I miss the small-town feel and some of the friends that I left behind, but my overall gut instinct is never to return.

After moving around as a child from Georgia to Texas, California, then back, we ended up in Roswell, which is where I lived until I moved to Albuquerque in 1985. Today I call Albuquerque home.

These days, most people have heard of or know about Albuquerque, if for no other reason, the International Balloon Fiesta, and the food! Locals refer to Albuquerque as a big small town because everywhere you go, you know someone. My mom Kaye was also born in New Mexico. My stepdad, the man that raised me since I was 12 years old, was born in Iowa. He is the man I call Dad today, as I never did have a relationship with my biological dad after he beat me. I am tight with my biological dad's family, and I am grateful for their love. My mom looks like Marilyn Monroe. She is petite, has big boobs, and blonde hair.

I've always wanted to live in California. I have visited northern and southern California many times and feel that is where I truly belong, but here I am, living in the desert.

I am getting married next month to Jake, and it will be the second marriage for both of us. I met him through a friend. It has been a slow process. Neither of us was in a hurry to get married again. Our exes are not who we should have been with, and our children are the only positive thing to have come out of those immature relationships.

Caleb, my son, is 17, almost 18, and Bailey, my daughter is 6. Her dad is Chris. Caleb's dad worked for my parents for many years. While we were on a family vacation in California, I found out I was pregnant. Caleb's dad was there with us, too. Although we decided not to marry each other, we tried to stay friends in the beginning. We had a history. He was part of our family and was always around our house before I got pregnant. We were young, and it was all about sex for us. Back then, I did not think about the consequences of not marrying Caleb's dad. Over the years, our relationship dwindled, and he has rarely been in touch with his son.

Caleb is a fantastic person. Not because he is my kid, but because he is genuinely a great person. The best decision I ever made in my life was to have my son. Believe me when I tell you it was not an easy life. I was alone. I had no partner to help me feel secure -- no partner to hold or love me when I hit the wall. And there were many nights I did just that.

Those early mornings and late-night feedings while struggling to be awake and present, I was alone. It was just my kid and me. At the beginning of Caleb's life, I did not even own a car. To get to and from daycare, then my school and a full-time job, I rode my 10-speed bike. As a tiny baby, I strapped my son into a carrier that was like a backpack. Luckily, that was temporary. With the help of my dad, I was able to get a car, which improved the safety of our lives drastically.

As evidenced by my awful choices and disgusting truths, I was living my truth; albeit screwed up. I realized who I was as I lay on my kitchen floor. After I stopped breastfeeding Caleb at nine months, I put him on a bottle. Exhaustion was all I knew. I boiled water to heat his bottle and thought I could rest my eyes for a minute or two while it got warm. I woke up to the horrible screech coming from the smoke detector.

The stove was on fire. As I reached for the pot the bottle was in, the palm of my hand was singed. I grabbed another pot to fill with water. As I threw it on the stove, half of it went on the floor, which is what caused me to slip and fall.

The fire was a debacle on a grand scale. I never did that again, and the stove always had evidence of a fire on top of it, a reminder for me to try to make better choices. I would have dwelled on my inadequacies and self-loathing had I had more time.

The degree of my stress and acute sense of my circumstances caused me to *not* be able to deal with my botched-up mess of a life. Not at that time anyway! On top of everything else, my mom made me feel like shit. She quickly reminded me *they* owned my house and the stove.

In 1981, just as I was coming to terms with being a whopping six months pregnant, my parents purchased 114 Wildy for us. An inexpensive (I think it was $23,000) small two-bedroom one bath house with a carport, front and back grassed yard and rose bushes. I loved it. Buying it put them in a better tax position; they needed the deduction. I was grateful to have an actual house to bring my child home to. My grandmother moved into the house when I moved to Albuquerque with Caleb when he was a toddler. After my grandma moved to Kosciusko, Mississippi, they sold it. If you google the address today, it is a dump. In fact, the entire street looks like an abandoned landfill.

For many years, I made one wrong decision after another while raising Caleb and trying to grow up myself. I knew nothing about raising a child. My mom did not make it easy for me, either. She regularly said, "You made your bed, now lie in it." I have never understood that screwed up logic.

When Caleb was three or four, I began to struggle with guilt about the possibility of ruining his life, especially since I had decided not to marry his dad. I was adamant about the fact I *chose* him and would raise him alone, and he would always know I loved him. Another huge lesson I learned after having him was about selfishness.

I have a ton of character flaws, but selfishness is not typically one of them. I sacrifice to the point of stupidity, and *not* because I am a martyr. Although I was very young when I had him, I knew my partying life had to end. Caleb was my priority.

I loved my baby and tried very hard not to screw up his life. I hoped I would get better at parenting, and eventually, I think I did. BUT there were many screwups along the way that will haunt me for the rest of my life. At times, I went against my own determination to put him first. In moments of selfishness, I did what I wanted to do.

Once again, the universe would slap me in the face to teach me another lesson. Caleb's calm demeanor started when he was a baby, and maybe it was because it was only, he and I. He could feel my tension and anxiety and would behave accordingly. I did not demand it. That was who he was and who he would grow up to be—a calm person.

When Caleb graduates from high school next month, he will leave home for the first time to attend a college in Colorado. He has earned a partial athletic scholarship to play baseball. To show Caleb how proud I am of him for graduating from high school, I bought him a used Ford Ranger as a graduation present. In hindsight, I am not sure what I was thinking at the time; it does not have air conditioning, and it is a tight fit because he is 6'2." The cab of the truck is small. Aubrey is seven, and Nicole is nine. They are Jake's kids. After Caleb leaves for school, we will have a six-, seven-, and nine-year-old at home!

Today, I have been running around completing our wedding plans and getting ready for Caleb's Senior Prom, which is later tonight. I plan to drive up to Colorado with Caleb a few days after his graduation. Caleb and I are close, and I will miss him, and I am confident he will miss me, too, but he will never admit it.

As I am getting ready to leave for work, Caleb yells out to me, "Mom, I am still packing, trying to decide what I am taking to school and what I am leaving here in my room. Can you stop and pick up the tux on your way home?"

"Yes, I will pick it up when I leave work later, which will be around 4:30 p.m. Will that work?"

He mumbles a "Yes" and asks me if I remembered to make Laura's corsage.

"Yes, I will bring it with me when I come home."

Several hours later, Caleb calls me, "Mom, where are you? I thought you would be here by now."

"I have plenty of time. I am leaving the kitchen now."

"Mom, hurry."

I shout out to anyone that is listening that I am leaving for the day. My yells go unanswered, and 45 minutes later, as I drive into the garage, Caleb is standing at the door with an irritated look on his face.

"Thank God, you are home, finally!"

Five minutes later, as I open a bottle of wine, I hear Caleb screaming. He is not wearing a shirt, only black socks, and his Tuxedo pants when he comes sliding around the corner on the hardwood floors.

"Caleb, what the hell is going on?"

He blurts out, "Look!"

About that time, my eyes finally meet up with his knees. I burst out laughing, which infuriates him. "What happened; how did your pants get that short?"

"I guess the jerks at that tux store messed up; I don't know, Mom!"

I scramble for the ticket so I can call them, but it is in his room somewhere, so I make my way as quickly as I can to retrieve it. While dialing the number, I am standing there, shaking my head, trying not to laugh. It is funny, but I know Caleb does not find the humor in this. He is already a nervous wreck, as this is his first real date.

I explain to the clerk on the other end of the line how we had rented a tux for my son's Senior Prom, and when we got home, we discovered the pants were not right. I explain that it's not a minor issue, and my son cannot wear the pants because they only come up to his knees!

Twenty minutes or so later, I am given the replacement tux and make a run for my car. The drive back home will take me another 15 minutes in traffic. I see Laura's family pulling into our subdivision just as I am pulling into our driveway.

"Caleb, I am home, and they are not charging us if that helps at all."

"Not really, Mom, but thanks!"

I love sarcasm in the middle of a crisis! I know our doorbell will ring any minute now, but I am desperate for a glass of wine. Just as I finished pouring a drink, the bell rings. Laura and her parents come in, and we make small talk in the kitchen while waiting for Caleb to enter. Caleb appears just as we were getting to know each other a little better. We force our children into positions for taking pictures. "Stand here. No, stand this way; please smile."

After about 10 minutes, I suspect the kids want to get as far away from us as possible. In pure vulture form, we follow them outside to continue snapping more pictures as they get into his truck. Then the tears come. They always do.

"Caleb, I love you, honey." He doesn't respond — little shit.

With that, Laura's parents leave, too, and I go back inside. I decide I will take my bottle of wine upstairs and sit out on the deck. The sun will set soon, and I can't think of a better way to end a stressful day.

A few weeks later, graduation has come and gone, and we are ready to make the trip up to Colorado. Jake and I are in the kitchen cooking breakfast. Making breakfast has always been a tradition in my family, and it's usually a big deal for us: potatoes with green Chile and cheese, sourdough pancakes or gooey French toast, eggs, bacon. The works.

It saddens me that Caleb will not be here on the weekends, or here much at all other than holidays and maybe during summer break. Just then, my thoughts dissolve as Bailey bursts into the kitchen. She is crying and saying she will miss her brother, and she doesn't know why he can't stay here.

"Oh, honey, I know you will miss Caleb, but he will always be your big brother, and he will always love you. I promise you; he will be back home soon."

I ask her if she is ready for a pancake, and with that, there are no more tears. How I wish a pancake could stop my tears as quickly. Early the next morning, the cars are loaded up, and we are ready to leave for Colorado. Bailey cries again, and Caleb assures her he will see her real soon.

"Bailey, I will be home when Mom and Jake get married. Can you wait that long, honey?"

Bailey hugs him so hard that when he pulls himself up from leaning over, she is attached to his neck. Caleb hugs her tight before dropping her. With that, we are on our way. Finally, and after several hours of driving, we get to the dorm. After a quick meet and greet with the new roommates, we unload the cars. Once done, we head off to Walmart to stock up on food and toiletries.

The buggy is overflowing, and I wonder how long this stuff will last him, and will he be able to keep it from his room-mates, or will they share? How will that work? We make it to school, unpack the groceries, and now I must leave my son and begin the drive home alone. I should be more mature, but I am not. In my excitement for Caleb to start this new chapter of his life, I'd forgotten about the part of the trip where I leave him.

I have stalled long enough and need to leave, but I don't want to. He is my real baby. We grew up together, and now I need to let him live his own life – on his terms.

Here it goes: "I love you, honey, and if you need—"

"Mom, stop crying, please; I will see you soon, and I am fine."

"Caleb, if you need anything, just call me, okay."

I hugged him and felt embarrassed for crying; his new roommates know neither of us and are watching this whole awkward scene. Strangers. Young and immature. Laughing at us. I walk outside and head toward the car, praying with each step that he doesn't call out or make me return. I am crying like a baby. And when I say crying, what I mean is big wallop of tears followed by strange noises leaping out of my throat — real ugly crying.

Caleb does call out, and I am afraid to turn around, but I do because I can't **NOT** turn around. I love this kid so much!

When he sees my face, he knows and says, "I love you, Mom, and thank you for everything."

Do all parents go through this when their child moves out for the first time? Once in my car, I search for a good radio station and drive away. After sobbing for most of the drive home, I finally had it together as I pulled into the garage at 1:40 a.m.

CHAPTER 3 – WEDDING DAY

As I lay looking up at the ceiling while clearing the goop in my eyes after a restful sleep, I am feeling optimistic. May in Albuquerque can be beautiful, but it can also rain and have severe wind and thunderstorms. Today, the weather report is calling for rain for the next week or so, but I choose to focus on the details of our wedding instead of the weather. Another issue at hand is we do not have anyone to marry us, and I do not have a dress yet.

All minor problems - right! Mom and I plan to leave work early today and try to find the dress. Aunt Myra has offered her home and her lovely backyard for our wedding. As if that was not enough, she insisted on making the wedding cake, too! We decided to make the food, flower arrangements, corsages, boutonnieres, and my bouquet ourselves. Aunt Myra has leukemia, and although she has a lot of energy, she does still have cancer. She lives with an appreciation for life, which makes anyone that knows her love her! For years, I have been curious how it is that my aunt has only been intimate with *one* man her entire life— her husband! She is a saint!

Caleb is planning on getting into town the day before the wedding, and it feels more like a reality now. Bailey broke her arm at school last week, so she is sporting a green and yellow-striped cast. She and Jake's daughter are the flower girls. They will each have a smaller bouquet and will carry a sweet, little, sequined bag that will hold our rings. Caleb will walk me out to the backyard, and Jake and I will get married under the newly constructed pergola.

Initially, Jake wanted us to go to Vegas and get "hitched." I objected. We are bringing up our four kids together, and we need to make them feel like they are our first love. It is not just about Jake and me. Mom calls and tells me she has great news.

"What?" I ask.

"We may have a judge to marry you now."

"What, how did that happen, Mom?"

"Last night, a judge who was a guest at the wedding, backed into one of the catering vans. I told him I would not file an insurance claim as long as he would agree to marry my daughter on Saturday."

"And?"

"He agreed."

"Cool, thanks, Mom. Let's hope he shows up."

Mom tells me, "If he doesn't show up, we have a back-up plan. Julie is planning on going online so she can get ordained or whatever it is to be able to marry people in New Mexico."

My favorite flowers are *roses*, *lavender*, and *stock* in every color. My plan is to arrange the flowers in various shapes and sizes of vases; including a couple of large mason jars too. Our wedding day is well on its way now, although it is about to rain. The forecast from earlier in the week was accurate! Damn the universe! Mom stopped at the local grower's market on her way to the kitchen. She bought fresh herbs, as well as an assortment of locally grown red onions, portobello mushrooms, squash, zucchini, and red and yellow peppers.

Carlos is about to start cooking the pork tenderloin. He has been instructed to grill each tenderloin on high heat, then slather raspberry chipotle generously all over them before putting in the oven. The wedding menu is as follows:

APPETIZERS:

Jarlsberg, caramelized onion and caraway phyllo triangles

Roasted corn, green Chile, and cacique cotija cheese quesadillas

Mini cheese pastry shells filled with a mixture of crab,

avocado, pineapple, and curry topped with toasted coconut.

DINNER:

Salad of arugula, watermelon, chevre and candied walnuts with mango lime vinaigrette

Raspberry chipotle glazed pork tenderloin

Heart attack potatoes infused with leek and fresh herbs

Roasted summer vegetables, drizzled with reduced balsamic

A variety of breadbaskets served family-style with olive oil and butter on the side.

To my surprise, Aunt Myra made three cakes! The main wedding cake is lemon thyme, which is topped with lemon-infused white chocolate curls, candied lemon wedges, and decorated with the palest, fresh yellow roses. Lemon-yellow everything! The second is carrot and walnut topped with sugar flowers and velvety cream cheese frosting. Coppery-colored real roses are the finishing touch. Jake's cake is a decadent Kahlua chocolate covered in silky ganache. She topped it with dark chocolate, raspberry, pistachio, and salted caramel flavored truffles.

Julie tells me she has her certificate from a 10-minute online course and will marry us if the judge fails to show up. I am surprised but also blown away by my family. They have stepped up to the plate with my wedding. I am a little concerned when I hear the doorbell ring, as it is too early for guests.

Caleb comes in to tell me, "Mom, the judge is here."

He is both charming and handsome. Very handsome. Jake offers him a glass of wine, which he gladly accepts. Finally, everyone is dressed and ready to greet our guests who seem to be filing in very slowly.

Initially, the reception was going to be outside, but earlier today, my uncle decided to move it indoors because we received such a downpour, the grounds are soaked. Hopefully, after the quick ceremony, the reception can begin on the patio and then move into the house for dinner. Thank goodness, my aunt and uncle's beautiful adobe home has a large great room that will accommodate us. As far as I know, everyone enjoyed themselves. Purposely, we only had our closest friends and family here today, which made it very intimate.

Our housekeeper, Zulema, whose name means "peace" in Spanish, plans to arrive early tomorrow to clean up the mess from today, so I do not have to think about it again. We do not have time for a real honeymoon, but we are going to a beautiful local resort for a couple of days.

The resort has three pools, and we plan on spending as much time as possible, laying out, swimming, drinking, and enjoying our new life. You know, everything we can do, crammed into three days! Mom is keeping the kids for us, and Caleb is getting an early start on driving back to school.

C HAPTER 4 – ONE LONG ROAD TRIP

Yesterday we made over a thousand meatballs for the up-coming weekend's events. Our meatballs are addictive. We typically will make several hundred or so at a time. After dumping all the ingredients into a large bowl, we roll and bake 'til almost done. Then the real magic happens. They swim in a red chili wine sauce, which contains the simple ingredients of cocktail sauce (the kind most people use when eating shrimp), a medium-priced bottle of Merlot, salt, pepper, and bay leaf.

Another aspect of Carlos' job is to clean and maintain the kitchen and the catering vans. He does a great job, despite the dumb servers that trash them out. I have never understood this. Mom is a perfectionist and demands organization and cleanliness, but the idiots that work for us continue to do the most stupid things imaginable. Don't get me wrong; I appreciate most of our regular servers. It is the newer, younger ones that drive me crazy!

One of the idiots called in a few days ago:

"I didn't load the van," is the first thing out of this twit's mouth, followed by, "It wasn't my fault."

I ask her if she pulled over before calling me. She tells me in a whiny, whimpering voice, "Yes, I pulled over, but I am in the middle of the road . . . kind of by the median, is that okay?"

I think to myself, 'Oh Lord, who raised your sorry ass!'

She further states, "The only issue is the meatballs are rolling around on the van floor."

Hmmm, that is **NOT** the only issue here! Naturally, I am more worried about the sauce, so I ask her about it.

She blurts out, "Well, yeah, Denine, of course, the sauce is all over the place, did you think the meatballs flew out without the sauce?"

No matter how you train your staff to load and unload the vans for off-site catering, they don't listen. They show up acting like they have not eaten for days, are scattered, hungover, and waiting for guidance from us. Did I say hungry? Every time they come to work, they act like it's their first time here, and they are always hungry!

Even though we have been through the same process over and over, it is rare to find someone that listens and genuinely wants to do a great job. When we see that diamond in the rough, we will move mountains for them to accommodate their schedule as much as possible.

Washing dishes is our break. We can hide back in the corner, absent of any voices but the ones in our heads. We have commercial dishwashers, but with catering trays that are larger than a healthy toddler, to stock pans that are two feet tall, some items cannot go through the dishwasher. And don't get me started on cleaning those chaffing pans, large trays, and serving platters. I hate that part of it. Of course, Mom wants every nook and cranny to be spotless, which makes it a more critical task. I will gladly clean toilets and wash dishes ahead of chaffers any day of the week!

Mom is a self-taught chef. I attribute her success to the fact that she loves food, and over the years, has learned what ingredients go best together. For example, a staple in our home is freshly chopped garlic, roasted green Chile, olive oil, and salt. We keep this in our fridge year-round and put heaping spoonful's on crackers or warm flour tortillas. You cannot get enough of it. Add cream cheese, and you have the makings of a tortilla pinwheel.

As a kid and through my early twenties, my parents owned and operated an FBO. What is an FBO? It stands for a Fixed-Based Operation. It's an aviation business that includes chartered flights, fuel, and maintenance for airplanes. They realized there was a need to provide good quality food for long journeys. Customers would ask, "Do you know any good restaurants nearby or any catering companies we could order food from?" The idea of Mom starting her own catering company was born of necessity. There was no one else at the time who could do it.

Mom would say, "Yes, I could make some food for you," which initially consisted of sandwiches, vegetable, and fruit trays. Only a short time later, Mom catered her first real event. It was a fantastic "end-of-training" party for Lufthansa, who had been training for a couple of months at our facility in Roswell.

The table and serving platters always decorated with fresh herbs and flowers. Today, we still decorate the food trays and tables with fresh flowers, fresh whole fruits, and herbs. For years, Mom catered for friends and close business associates, as well as the many corporations that trained out at the airport.

Mom did not come from money, nor did she have it for a large portion of her early life, so she is thrifty and creative. When she married my stepdad, he didn't have much of anything either, but they brought out the best in one another. A short amount of time passed after they married before they were able to buy their first house.

Together. Neither of them had ever purchased a house, so this was a big thing in our family, back when buying a home meant something. Even with perfect credit, the interest rate in the 1970s was high, and they had to save for the down payment. I knew that then, and I understand it now.

My mom's parents lived in Alabama for a large portion of her childhood. Suffice it to say, they lived in the sticks, and Mom could not wait to leave home. Her desire to leave home had nothing to do with geography. Although she has a few fond memories of parts of her childhood, her mind is riddled with sadness and trauma that was brought on by the effects of poverty and alcoholism. She has never dwelled on it, but it left her wanting a better life.

My grandfather worked in the oil fields, which meant the family frequently had to move from town to town. Maybe that

LIFE BEYOND THE KITCHEN DOOR

explains why, at times, he could be mean. It kills me when I hear how he frequently mistreated my Uncle Gary. My favorite uncle! Grandpa's anger reached much farther than a punch to the face would have. Physical pain might have been better. Verbal abuse is awful; mean words linger around long after bruises heal. The myriad of horrifically harsh words screamed at him, left deep scars.

Mom told us kids about Grandpa being racist, too. He yelled at her after she picked cotton all day in the scorching Alabama sun, "I better not see you with that son of a bitch nigger again." I don't think Grandpa was inherently racist; I believe he was socially retarded from growing up in the South during a time when people were very divided, and some lacked common sense. Luckily, I never saw grandpa act like that.

No doubt, Deb and I got our rebellious streaks from Mom, and today, none of us could fathom being racist or prejudiced. She would ignore Grandpa by deliberately going to visit her friend that lived across the ditch. Mom loved her and did not see color or difference. She was just as poor and loved my mom, too. Mom's defiance enraged Grandpa. Once Mom figured out that her younger brother Gary would take the brunt of "her" punishment – even though he was never involved – she had no choice but to forget about her friend.

Anyway, they moved a lot because they had to go where there was work. Mom and Gary were never able to finish even one entire school year in one school. I think it made them both very strong. To say her life has been one long "road trip" is an understatement. New house. New town. New school. Maybe a new friend.

Mom and Uncle Gary have told me stories about how they would abruptly "up and move." They were instructed to pack their clothes and shoes, and if they were lucky, they could take a toy or two. That's if they even had a toy at that time! If the car and small trailer were full, then they had to leave behind everything else. And that was how each road trip began and ended.

To say it was a casually cruel existence would be an

understatement. Even if they would not understand it until they were older, there was trauma in their lives. Grandpa eventually left the oil fields for a job in the union as an ironworker. The position brought stability and steady income.

Luckily, their younger siblings did not experience the same disrupted life, but they did live with an alcoholic parent with a propensity for fighting in bars and running around with other women. My uncle's attempt to run from my grandpa's abuse led him to join the army. He was underage, so my grandmother signed for him. Out of desperation, he "ran away" to fight in the Vietnam War. And my mom ran into the arms of my father.

After hearing the stories about their upbringing, it is nothing short of a miracle they survived at all. As an adult, I now know exactly why they were able to survive. They each had a fire deep inside that was fueled by a *need* to live a good life.

Mom is not bitter, and if you asked her today how she survived it, she would tell you, "That is all we knew, and it was normal to us at the time. We had dirt floors but didn't know we were dirt poor."

I loved my grandparents. Grandpa drank until the day he died, but Grandma never did. Grandma's one vice was smoking. She was a tall, slender woman with short brownish hair. She was pretty and had a simple way about her. She was kind and always careful about what came out of her mouth. If I close my eyes, I can still see her standing at the stove.

I would cringe as I watched and waited for the ashes to fall from her cigarette into the pot of beans. They always seemed to grow to at least an inch long before they fell. They regularly did fall into the pot, but it never stopped us from eating whatever she had cooked. Grandma was an excellent cook. Grandma frequently cooked a pot of beans, fried potatoes with yellow onion, cornbread in an iron skillet, and maybe a pork chop if there was extra money that week. It seemed like we always had garden tomatoes and cantaloupe, too, at every meal. I feel this is a Southern tradition.

As a child and a grandchild, life was good. I have often wondered if my mom found her love of cooking from watching her mom.

C HAPTER 5 – MARLBORO MAN AND MARGARITAS

After only a few months into our marriage, I certainly feel like I married up. I still remember the gigantic Marlboro man billboard from when I was a teenager. My friends and I dreamed of marrying him when we grew up. In my eyes, Jake is my Marlboro man. Sexy as hell in so many ways. He looks like Dennis Quaid, loves everything about the outdoors, and is always wanting to have a good time. So, although Jake is a handsome man, he is also my soul mate in every way. He gets me and understands that I will never "look" like his best counterpart.

Only on rare occasions does he see me pulled together, looking like what you would call hot! He accepts that, and I love him for it. We almost didn't get married to each other. When we first met, I was dating someone else and pushing him to date a then friend of mine. At the time, I respected and thought highly of her. I felt they would be a good match, but I was wrong. Only a few weeks after they started dating, Jake learned she had met a "friend" for a drink. In his mind, if she could do that, he wondered what else she might be capable of doing.

It left a bad taste in his mouth, like the other cheaters in his past. My grandma's name for that kind of women was "hussy." This description would have fit me as well during different times in my life.

Another thing -- she pushed hard to sleep with Jake. Like right away. Believe it or not, that too was a turn-off. It wasn't like they were horny teenagers that "had" to have sex! As it turned out, she was not who we thought she was as a person, and Jake and I found our way to each other.

I have a reputation for being a little too "quick and dirty." I take shortcuts to get as much work done as possible, and this is always my mode of operation. It's a bad habit I learned from watching my mom. Today, I regret this trait. I feel that had I been taught a different way of life; I would have been equipped to make more sound decisions. Or, maybe the lessons I have learned through living a difficult life, is why I am who I am now.

Slowly, I am learning more about myself. I am a risk-taker and occasionally lack common sense. Jake, however, walks in fear. It keeps him grounded; so, by association, I am finally learning a new way to live. We balance each other.

When I was still single, I purchased this house after the real estate market started to dive. Although financially speaking, it was a great deal, I find I have never appreciated the beauty of our home and by extension, the view – that is, until today.

While contemplating my day, coffee in hand, I, along with our sad chocolate Labrador Maya, make our way upstairs and out to the deck. The view is the best part of this house. How could I have forgotten the magnificence from up here? Upstairs, we have a margarita deck. I am not sure who came up with that, but it works for me. We are margarita connoisseurs, especially Jake, who is our resident mixologist. He loves to incorporate fresh juices of all kinds.

Simply put; a splash of this, a dash of that! For a splendid margarita, you only need a couple of ingredients: tequila, lime, and juice. Any variation will work. I love Cointreau in mine. I learned that from Mom, who is the original margarita specialist in our family.

Maya is the beautiful chocolate Lab that we rescued three years ago. She was severely abused while in the care of so-called dog lovers. When she first came to live with us, we worked hard at helping her calm down. She is terrified of thunder and any loud noise. Maybe it's a Lab thing, but she always looks sad. I believe she is happy living with us, and I wish that she could overcome her past and learn we will not hurt her.

This past Sunday, we finished putting the house back together after another year of celebrating Thanksgiving and our family "feast-a-thon." The weatherman said today would be the coldest day of the year so far, which I tend to agree with, as the external thermostat reads a chilly 28 degrees. The snow on the rooftop across the street has not melted all day- not even since the last snowfall, which was over a week ago.

Beyond our neighbor's roof are the majestic Sandia Mountains. They appear to be larger than life, and as the New Mexico sun starts to set in the west, the glow reflecting on the *Sandia*, which means watermelon in Spanish, is brilliant.

I have been working alongside my mom for over 18 years in the catering business. The food business *sounds* glamorous, but it is one of the hardest jobs you can do. It is simultaneously rewarding and challenging. I always ask myself if we are crazy. Do we employ crazy and whacked-out people? Or maybe just alcoholics, drug addicts, and ex-cons?

In this business, you must devote yourself to long hours and work in cramped, sometimes terrible working conditions. I cannot count how many holidays and birthdays I have either missed or been late to in my own family. Why would anyone choose this profession? Did something go wrong in our DNA? Did something go wrong in their DNA, which led them to us and to beg to be part of this crazy life?

My Aunt Myra has always told me that my energy and the energy in our business is infectious. For as long as I can remember, we have hired people from the information found on little yellow office "stickies" instead of using employment applications. Over time, the yellow stickies would suddenly have a scribble of a flower or some other picture. We identified them by the scribbles, an indication we either liked them or didn't want them to work with us. "Please write your name and telephone number down on the sticky and leave it on the desk; if we are interested, we will call you." Which translates to, "If we are desperate, we will call you for sure!"

Anyone in the food business knows there are times that you hire just about anyone when you're desperate to have another set of hands! That is our norm, and to this day, that is how we hire people. For the most part, it has not failed us, as we have employees that have worked here almost as long as I have.

Carlos is one of those employees. He is from Mexico and is legal, but his family is not. His **beloved** (his word) is from Mexico, and their two children are U.S. citizens. She is paranoid about everything to do with our kitchen. She even accuses Carlos of sleeping around with the beautiful servers. Mom and I will never forget something he told us. He was having a rough time with his beloved. One morning he came in, wringing his hands. He was a mess. He said his beloved demanded to smell his "chorts" (shorts) when he got home from working yesterday – He further stated she said, "if I smell a woman or you smell different down there, then you're caught." I do not think either of us will ever get that image out of our heads.

There *is* a lot of sex that goes on in the food business, lots of drinking, smoking, and more sex. That is also the norm. However, sex with Carlos would never happen, and his wife has no reason to worry. Not about this. No one that works for us would ever sleep with him!

Carlos is an employee we can count on 24/7. He is about five feet tall and kind of on the thin side. Of course, all of us women tower over him. We look like giants when we are working side by side next to Carlos. Over the years, there have been times when I have wanted to slap the shit out of him. I must admit that during long days, fantasizing about chopping him up into little bits makes the time go by quicker.

Carlos is strong and can stay on task for hours. He and I have both stood at the same prep table for 10 hours at a time, either making a thousand green Chile, chicken, and corn flautas or making bacon-wrapped dates by the hundreds. You name it; we have made it. Everything made from scratch. No packaged food of any kind. Fresh and organic wherever possible. Working long hours together is why we know our employees so well. We spend more time with each other than with our own families.

You cannot always trust the food vendors, so we make

many trips to our local farm stands and even specialty stores. Our drive to serve the freshest food is what has made our company so successful. However, very time consuming and sometimes stretches us beyond our limits. Last year, I was running into our neighborhood grocery store in the middle of summer. As per usual, we were behind schedule, and I was in a big hurry.

The store is located only a few blocks from our kitchen, but it still takes time to get there and back. As I was running into the store, I noticed a cool old truck. I remember thinking it was from the '50s, turquoise, and kind of rusted out, yet it looked reliable.

The old guy driving the truck heard his wife tell him, "Stop, there is someone back there." However, instead of the brakes, he hit the gas pedal and backed up over me. Just barely, but it knocked me down. The worst part was the scorching fire poker hot asphalt full of little sharp pebbles. It was hot; it felt like being in the belly of a volcano -- that hot!

The heat coming from the parking lot asphalt singed my legs as I lay there absent of any thought regarding the "coolness" of that old truck. I was wearing shorts, and I had road-rash from here to breakfast. My shoulder looked like I had been "skinned" with a sharp knife. It hurt like hell! In the background, I could hear people yelling out. A nice guy that worked there helped pull me out from under the back end of the truck so that I could get back on my feet.

"Lady, you are bleeding, do you need an ambulance?"

"No, I got it. I am in a hurry and got to run. I'm fine." (You know me -- "down and dirty" gets it done.)

By now, the old guy and his wife are trying to determine if I plan on suing. She is visibly upset and assures me they will take care of any medical bills. Poor old man. She is screaming at him!

"You, idiot, I told you not to back up."

I assured them that I would not sue them, and I did not need to go to the hospital. They asked me my name and why I was in such a hurry. I told them we had a wedding to prepare for and two other dinner parties.

"I work for a catering company up the road, and I am running late, so we are good, I am fine."

Mrs. "Cool Truck" begged me to let her come help me. She repeated, "Honey, I learned to cook while working at the family farm. I work hard, and I will not get in your way."

I assured her that I had enough help and thanked her. Somehow, as I drove out of the parking lot, I felt guilty for not letting her come to help us.

C HAPTER 6 – MONKEY SEE, MONKEY DO

My sister is married to an asshole, Russell. He wasn't always a jerk, but after my sister got sick, he lost his nerve to stay engaged in their life. They have two children, Ana, and Meaghan. Ana is Russell's biological daughter from a previous marriage, and Meaghan is Deb's daughter from an earlier marriage. Ana is 20, and Meaghan just turned 18.

Deb fell in love with Ana immediately, and we all treat her the same way we treat Meaghan, with tons of love and acceptance. I do not think I have ever heard Deb use the word "stepdaughter."

Ana has a son Isaac who will turn two next month, and Meaghan works with us in the kitchen. She will make a great chef one day, as she loves to cook — it is also in her DNA, her "sickness." Ana started taking college classes while she was in high school and will graduate from nursing school in the Fall.

Deb and I have a love-hate relationship, not unlike most sisters. For most of our lives, we have been inseparable. Love, fight, makeup, fight again, repeat. We have differences in our clothing style, hairstyle, mannerisms, and so on. Deb has strawberry blonde hair, freckles everywhere, and piercing, beautiful blue eyes. As teenagers, we bantered back and forth.

Her periods were just awful. Or so she would say. Each month — terrible. To which I replied, "bullshit." Mine were a breeze, and I barely noticed them at all – after being traumatized with my first one, believe me, I paid attention. She used her periods as an excuse not to have to participate in gym class at school. Mom absentmindedly wrote one excuse after another for her so she could skip it altogether.

Deb has always been busty, and in my opinion, she didn't like the idea of wearing a bra and undressing in front of the flat-chested girls at school. She called me a "goody-two-shoes" for years. It took her a lifetime to realize I wasn't one; I was acting out from my position in the family — the middle child position. When Matt and I returned from our visit with our bio dad – after my beating and foster care, she treated me differently. She was my protector. If anyone tried to hurt me, they had to go through her.

We grew up more like twins, and when we were super little, Mom would dress us alike. Deb has always been the one in the family to love reading, too. She enjoyed reading aloud to us, which transported us to new and thrilling adventures. We held onto secrets. I had hers, and she had mine. It was as if we had written them down on paper; then swallowed them. No one would ever know what *we* knew! Not even Matt. Together, Deb and I did our best to protect Matt when he was younger, too. That feeling has stuck with me, a position I strive for often. I do not want to see him suffer on any level!

The smell of rubbing alcohol always takes me back to when Deb and I, without permission from our mother, pierced our ears. As teens, we questioned authority and rebelled often. The punishment was always worth it.

I am the family Mexican with olive skin, brown eyes, and brown hair. Although I pride myself on having a big heart, I battle with my emotions, which are unsettling. I loathe self-pity and under no circumstance is playing a victim ever okay. Matt and Jason both have fair skin—but Matt tans in the summer and has green eyes and brown hair. Jason has green eyes, blond hair, and is very white, and is our half-brother; his dad is our stepdad.

Matt and Jason have both worked in the business at different times. Matt works mostly as a server at events, but Jason is an excellent cook and works with us full time now. That, too, has its issues!

I could tell you several stories about Jason and me fighting in the kitchen. After all, he was the "man," and I was just

Denine — the middle kid. I do not want you to think badly of Jason, as he is a cool brother and a great person, but he and I could easily clash when we worked together.

I spent the early years working with Mom when she was building up the business, so maybe that was the *real* issue. I felt I had paid my dues, so to speak, and was an integral part of the company. It was I who worked beside Mom every day. At times, we worked 18-hour days for years! In the beginning, Mom would dictate, and I would type the menus.

After several years, I became an expert at menu design as well, because I understood what it meant to take it from the paper stage to the reality of making and serving it. She and I have laughed our butts off at what we fondly call "Creative Writing 101." At times, maybe I have resented Jason as much as he disliked my position in the business.

As the middle child, I try to keep the peace as much as I can, but there are days when this is impossible. On one such occasion, and while Mom was out of town, Jason and I had been working long days, and our tempers were flaring. I did not like the way he prepped and cooked, and he thought I was an idiot.

Other than eating, food has never meant as much to me as it does to my other family members. All I ever knew was that our family had great cooks, and we never ate a bad meal. I have learned to cook and am pretty good at it. More importantly, I have improved over the years. However, it is not what drives me.

While catering, I have embraced the experiential and creative design part of it. Figuring out cool and edgy decorating ideas along with great venue locations gets me excited. We made the mashed potato bar cool long before it was popular. You start with piping hot mashed potatoes. Good potatoes too! We add real butter, cream cheese, and heavy whipping cream — garlic, salt, and pepper also. Then we serve with varieties of toppings like gravy, gruyere cheese, scallions, or caviar and serve them in martini glasses with a small spoon.

Therefore, when I say I am a monkey, what I mean is "monkey see, monkey do." I can watch and then follow any recipe you throw at me. I figure it out quickly. Jason, on the other hand, has a better idea of what goes together, so he is never afraid to combine ingredients or change recipes. Real or not, somehow, his confidence translates into my weakness.

On this day, I snap at Jason and tell him, "Mom does not cut the asparagus like that!"

He snaps right back and tells me, "She isn't here, and we are doing it my way, which is the right way. The days of snapping the ends of the asparagus are gone; we are too damned busy to do it like that, Denine." He would grab three bunches of asparagus at a time and whack the ends off.

The mindless whacking infuriated me. I understand the concept, and it does make more sense to do it fast like that, but it was in the way he scolded me that irritated me. He is not my boss today, or ever, for that matter. A few minutes into our heated discussion, the asparagus is flying all over the place. We were both throwing it, and I was livid.

It scares the shit out of Carlos, who quickly disappeared into the catering closet, a place we keep our serving trays, chaffers, props, and anything else we use for catering. We refer to the catering closet as the "hiding place," and we have all been there many times to get away from the drama in the kitchen. Tempers can be fast and furious in the kitchen. But luckily, they leave just as fast as they come! The next day or so, we were able to laugh about it.

Here is the deal with my brother, Matt. He is in prison. At 17, he started getting high. We all did. That was the norm. Not for Deb or Jason, but Matt and I have this in common. I never did it in excess, and it did not lead to anything stronger, but with Matt, sadly, it did. The first time he used meth, he was addicted. His best friend back then was Bobby, and it was him that first gave Matt the meth.

His addiction has kept him in and out of jail and prison for years. The sad thing is, he is a great person. I have always known it would take something dire for Matt to change his life.

I strongly disagree with our penal system regarding drug addiction. I am not talking about trafficking drugs, only the addiction side of it.

Bobby has also been in and out of prison; just like Matt, he has lost everything several times over. Family, kids, housing, cars. Everything that ever mattered anyway.

My first love was Bobby's cousin Jack. He was a perfect soul, full of life. Our families were friends and business associates. My parents were strict, so to be able to see each other; we would sneak around. Our family had a big, brown station wagon that I was *permitted* to drive, but I always had to take Jason with me. I would snap him into the seatbelt, and off we'd go.

They thought if I had a chaperone, I could not get into trouble. Geez, was that stupid! A kid chaperone. Imagine that for a second! The sneaking around made me a good liar. He was a little older than me, and my parents hated the fact that all I wanted in life was to be with Jack.

Jack was the coolest person I had ever met, so when he was interested in me too, I fell hard. He was always riding motorcycles and working on his car, and we would drive out to the mesa every chance we could, to make out. Once we were getting "hot and heavy" and didn't realize it had already turned dark. I knew my mom would lose her mind, but it was worth it. My bra was off, and Jack's hands were finding their way down my pants when suddenly there was a tap on the window. The officer told us to get our asses home and never to come back out there again.

A few weeks later and after pouting all day because I could not see him, I decided to go to a movie with a friend. Cathy is an extraordinary person. Kind-hearted, meek, and mild. It was not in her nature to cuss or gossip about anyone else. Opposite of me at that time. So, when she called, I accepted her offer and welcomed the distraction.

While getting ready, I heard the phone ring and thought it was Cathy. A few minutes later, Dad came into my room to tell me that Jack had been in an accident; "Denine, Jack died while riding his motorcycle."

I thought he must have been playing a cruel joke on me. I hated my dad for telling me like that – abruptly as if he was announcing Cathy's arrival or something. The pain of losing the love of my life was all-encompassing. All I felt was emptiness and sadness and did not want to go on living without him. His family treated me with kindness.

They did what they could to help me get through the pain, even though they were suffering. I begged his brother, who was the only person riding with him, to tell me what and how it happened. To this day, I never heard the details, and for that, I am grateful.

My thoughts back then were how calm his mom was and how much grace she displayed. She is a kind woman and has suffered many losses in her life since then. Jack's death must have changed her forever because I know how it changed me!

Our family physician made house calls. He and Dad were drinking buddies, so it didn't surprise me when he showed up to check on me after Jack died. You might expect a doctor to be wearing dress slacks or even hospital garb, but he wore jeans and leather flip-flops. I stayed semi-sedated for a few days. I did not want to live. I thought about suicide more than a dozen times. I wanted to stop breathing.

I was desperate to be able to laugh with Jack again and to be able to feel him hold my hand in his. My memories were all that kept me going.

Jack's parents had a cabin not far from where we lived. It was in their mountain cabin that I lost my virginity to him. It was a scary time for sure. I had no idea, absolutely no idea what was about to happen. For several months, we had been making out every chance we could but had never gone all the way.

I knew Jack knew what to do because he had told me that he had slept with a few other girls before me. We finally decided to do it, and if *it* was going to happen, I would have to run away from home!

Any consequence would be worth it to be able to have sex

with Jack! I had three close friends at that time in my life: Juli, Kellie, and Brenda. Juli and I went to the same high school and saw each other all the time. I lied and said I was spending the night with her.

She was my cover story.

Mom is not an easy person to talk to when it comes to relationships. I found it challenging to open-up to her.

She never even spoke to us about our periods. The day I got mine – luckily, I had just gotten home from school and was in my bedroom. It felt like I had wet my pants, but different. To say I was clueless is an understatement. If my health class covered this topic, I must have missed it altogether because I was in shock!

So much embarrassment! I grabbed Mom when I heard her walking down the hall near my room. To my surprise, she said she would take care of it, and it was normal. "You got your period; all women do." Okay, what the heck does that mean, I am not a woman yet. I thought to myself. I remember *that* day like it was yesterday. Etched in my memory- in *blood*!

It was probably only twenty minutes or so later, when my dad appeared in my room. More embarrassment at my expense.

He bought the largest purple box of Kotex pads I had ever seen. Like 2 feet tall and **purple**! Who in the world came up with designing that- probably a man! At first, I thought they were some type of a diaper. 'I know, IDOT – right!' Remember, I never had the "talk." I had seen the same box at my grandma's house, but never paid any attention to it.

The day before, Mom and I had been to the same grocery store that Dad went to. Today, I still remember the store was decorated for what they referred to as "Hawaiian Days." The checkers knew me and my family well. I avoided that store for as long as I could after Dad bought that ridiculous box of pads.

Mom, in fact, did not take care of it and I worked at being mad at her for months for not going to the store herself.

You and I know there had to have been, at a minimum, stares. I believe Mom said Dad told them he was not operating a brothel – *'laugh at my expense.'* **Denine started her period**.

To this day, so much embarrassment as a teenager! I didn't even know back then what a brothel was!

We were on our own when it came to our time of the month. Or other descriptors *"shark week, the red badge of courage, moon time, on the rag, and a visit from ... some aunt."* Our own language when it came to our menstruating. You get it; girls (not women) have been dealing with the starting of their period since the beginning of time.

Another memory about learning how to live with our "time of the month." My girlfriends were also experiencing the same awkwardness. About a year after we all started our periods, we joked about our inept parents. I was not the only girl that didn't have the puberty talk. To me, it wasn't in the how we should have discussed it; it was in the when!

My bedroom was located immediately next to my bathroom. It was accessible from the hallway and most of the time, I was the only one that used it. Occcasionally, Mom would sneak in and smoke in my bathroom. It had a window and she never knew we knew what she was doing. Little did she know, we used that window too!

Anyway, two of my friends came over one afternoon so we could collectively figure out how to use tampons. We had each failed on our own so thought we could figure it out together if we practiced.

Keep in mind, we were not on our periods and we knew little about our anatomy. An innocent and successful exploration accomplished in an hour. No longer dreading it, we excitedly looked forward to our next period where we could ditch the bulky pads. We outsmarted our parents; we knew everything.

During that same time in my life and before having sex, like most of my friends, I daydreamt about it. I was confident it would be like an out-of-body, beautiful, and magical experience. That somehow, once we did *it*, I would forever be a smarter person.

I *had* to be with Jack. He encouraged me to be honest with my mom, but she would never approve, and I felt more comfortable lying about my activity.

After losing my virginity, I remembered lying naked on the bed afterward and thinking, **this is it**. I was embarrassed and confused. It hurt like hell, and I wasn't sure how I would ever learn to enjoy sex. It was not magical at all!

When I missed the time that I was supposed to be back home, Mom went to Juli's house to get me. Of course, I was not there and had not been there all night. Later, when I got home, Mom punished me. I washed airplanes all summer and had to babysit Jason anytime they went out. I never made a dime that year. For days, all I heard was blah, blah, blah about how I had hurt them.

As far as I was concerned, they were only worried about their reputation with their wealthy friends and whether I could be trusted to watch Jason again. My response to her was, "only time will tell." Yes, I was a sarcastic teenager!

I had a good relationship with Jack's brother and his wife, and my love for her made my days bearable. After Jack died, we stayed close for many years. Rene frequently comes to help us with catering when we are busy, even today, as she is an accomplished cook herself.

Losing Jack prepared me for the many losses to come in my life. I am still in touch and feel great love for both Juli and Kellie, but I have not been in contact with Brenda since high school–a side effect of me making bad decisions at the expense of hurting others.

CHAPTER 7 – THE MIDDLE CHILD

Before my sister got sick, I was the middle child in every way. I wanted everyone to get along. I tried to be the family peacemaker. I thought if I could say something that would urge or sway another family member to back down or just change their stubbornness, then we could all be okay. As a middle child, from my perspective, everything was wrong.

My constant need to prove myself – my self-worth has been shadowing me – for my entire life. In hindsight, my rock bottom was really not rock bottom at all. It taught me to persevere. To keep pushing that rock up the steep and slick mountain of my screwed-up life. The exercise taught me that it (the rock) would fall and land smack dab on my face, but it was important to me to keep trying at life.

Why was I switched at birth, almost drown and ..... almost kidnapped - only to remain broken in this family? My life must mean something!

In the darkness of my soul, I knew I was here for a reason. It could not have been just a mistake or by chance! So, with each problem in my life, I try harder. Yes, I have family. Yes, I even have people that love me. But it has never been enough for me because I am never enough for them.

Early in my life, I fell short of acquiring that position. The men I loved never loved me the way I loved them. My friends never loved me the way I loved them. My family never loved me the way I loved them.

Gloom replaced the gaps of light in my life. Lessons were hard and at times; even dangerous. My brain was never the issue;

I am smart.

It was my heart. I wanted more. I wanted all of it! A normal family. Acceptance, unconditional love, self- confidence from a job well done. Approval from my parents that I was a good kid.

All grown up; I've been able to be honest. To see the world and my family in a more honest way. We do not all see life the same way and that is okay.

Thousands of mistakes have been made by all of us and we are not that family where generations of married and never divorced parents raised well balanced - sane children.

I am rarely, if ever, accepted in an unconditional manner. It feels like there are always strings attached. I no longer care about that damn rock - the "letting go" has allowed me much freedom.

Today, I recognize the fact that I am basically a shallow person. It is easy for me to compartmentalize my life. I can't spend time over-thinking it all. I lock things away in order to survive. It is not that I don't care. It is more the fact that I can only care so much!

Another huge lesson I learned has to do with the way I am treated. I finally learned that it has little to do with me and today, that brings me much peace.

When I started organizing my thoughts in order to write this book, a flash of a memory was forefront and it was a bad memory. Well, should I say memories!

There were two instances in my life where I was molested. One was a boyfriend of a neighbor and the other was someone within my family. Not related by blood, but he crossed the line in a huge destructive way.

I kept both of these abuses locked away in my heart. At eleven years old, why did I feel like I couldn't tell anyone?! Neither of the pigs threatened me in any manner. Why was I okay with silence? Why did I not want them punished? Did I feel like I deserved to be abused? That doesn't sound like me, but again - maybe that is when I learned to shut my emotions off in order to survive.

My mom has always known that I am the strong one. Much stronger than my siblings. Reality about family dynamics is clear. When you have vulnerable kids versus strong kids, the weaker takes precedence. The strong kid will be forced to "take one for the team" in order to make it easier for the family. But it comes at a huge price; paid by the strong kid. In my case, a life of feeling like the black sheep of the family. Not a good feeling at all.

I appreciate the fact that life is not "arms or legs." We have all suffered from the "arms and legs" of life. Today, I know what is and isn't important. How many of us have said, "If I had only known then what I know now?"

I guess surviving has different meanings for all of us. For me, it means family. I know if I give up at life, the collateral damage will be severe for those left behind. I never feel sorry for myself and I seem to find the silver lining to all problems.

What I *do* care about these days are my family and close friends. And if I have family members that do not like or care for me, I can't worry about it. I am always interested in my children and if they have good or bad days. I beg to hear about their triumphs and failures. I am excited when my son tells me he struck everyone out during a game. If a friend calls, I am excited to hear about what's new with them. These are the things that are important to me now.

I have changed.

I used to be a sweet girl. That girl has been gone for a very long time now. What's left is a broken shell of a woman fighting to put one foot in front of the other. If Jake and I fight, it is me that backs down. I want it over quickly.

Bruce was a friend of mine that lost his battle to cancer. He suffered, suffered a lot! Through it all, he maintained his dignity, which I believe was due to his strong faith in God. I stood in awe of his attitude. He lived with grace right through the very last day of his life, which set an example for his wife, children, grandchildren, and close friends. Bruce knew the difference in the "arms and legs of life" and fully understood that in life, what counts most is your relationships and how you live your life. He is no longer suffering, but those of us blessed to have been able to call him our friend miss him often.

Although it is taking me a long time to change my thought process, I made a promise to Bruce to stop cussing. My mouth is my curse. It is reckless and crass, but I am trying. Over the years and through the course of working so hard at being that "peacekeeper," I have lost a lot of myself.

When you spread yourself thin, no one gets anything but a few crumbs; you create hostility and teach your kids they do not come first. There have been times – lots of times that I put work first.

Every other event in my life came in second or third. The funny thing is I never like to disappoint or let anyone down, but I know I have hurt many people, and I am genuinely sorry for that. I do not feel sorry for myself. I am who I am, and although I am full of flaws, I do not spend time beating myself up over the mistakes. Each morning I wake up with a fresh outlook.

I have always wanted to be a parent and dreamt of having four or five kids. Sitting at a park watching them play was my perfect day. Now, I see it clearly. I should have planned my life better. So many people have been let down by me, although it was never my intention. We all know good intentions mean nothing.

The day my nephew was born, we had been working for several hours in the kitchen. It was a hot day, and the swamp cooler was not keeping us cool. It was a miserable day. Occasionally, we dunk our t-shirts under the water in hopes of cooling off. My excitement was too much to contain after I got the green light to run to the hospital. My brother, Jason's firstborn, had just been born, and I had to see him!

It was essential to let that little boy know how much he was loved and how we all longed to meet him. Once in the hospital, I made my way to the elevator. I could see from the look on other people's faces that I must smell bad or look dreadful. It was probably both, as I am wearing the same t-shirt from earlier in the day and a pair of shorts. The elevator stops at the baby floor first, and as I exit the elevator, I tell the "judgy" family to have a beautiful day. No response.

At the nurses' station, I ask permission to enter the nursery. One of the nurses looks at me somewhat strangely, like the way the elevator family looked at me. Now I am wondering what is up. About that time, Jason comes out and tells me I must get washed and gowned up before entering.

He looks at me and says, "Denine, you stink. What is that smell?"

I say, "It was pretty hot in the kitchen today."

"Well, you smell, fishy."

I forgot I had been working with fresh salmon all day. I stunk, and there was nothing I could do at that very moment. They would have to let me in! It was not beneath me to beg to see the new baby.

However, Jason saw my frustration, and lovingly said, "You're fine, come on back."

After holding that sweet baby for only a few minutes, I took my smelly body back to the kitchen. While driving, I was overcome with sadness because I would never get a second chance to hold that baby for the very first time. Again, I blew it. Although I wanted to celebrate my nephew's birth, I was on autopilot and just going through the motions. I was spreading myself too thin.

Mom told me the next day that Jason's wife, Cindy, was miffed at me. Suffice it to say, Cindy and I have never been close, but I do respect the fact that she is married to my brother and is the mother of his son. Deb has always been closer to Cindy, not me.

Back to reality and as usual. We are working at warp speed in the kitchen. This weekend we have seven events. Tomorrow we are catering an outdoor sit-down wedding for 500 guests. For this event, we will have to make a prep kitchen on site which will be a huge joint effort to accomplish. Viscerally and instinctively, I have learned that food is life. My life. I love this profession. It's stressful at times, but I still love it.

Our common ground in my family is the food and all that comes with it. Personally and professionally.

I crave the time we can sitdown together and share a meal. Any meal will do. It is and isn't about the food itself. Of course, we want the good stuff; made in our own homes taking great care in the makings of the meal, but sharing a delivery pizza works too. The time together teaches us about patience. Bringing lives together; one bite at a time. We love having friends over too. Our desire to feed people is linked to our DNA. Weddings, birthdays, funerals - it is appropriate at all times! Food may not be the reason we get together, but it always takes center stage - that is: food, wine, beer, margaritas and special fun cocktails! It is my belief we are creating memories that will sustain us when times get difficult.

Happiness, joy and sadness linked to the meal eaten while sharing that time together- I believe it can stabilize our hearts from living a hectic life.

After many years, we have carved out a charming life-style, but it is not absent of drama, burned and singed arms and red velvet welts covering body parts that one would never imagine could be burned.

We all show signs of burns and cuts from working in the kitchen. Some are minor, and some should have had stitches, or at a minimum, a trip to an urgent care center. Personally, my arms and hands are hideous looking from the burns; if we could take just one more minute to have located the first aid kit, then I am confident our stains and injury scars would not be as shocking.

Although we plan each event out well, often we get behind schedule and race around like chickens without their heads. Therefore, we can never take the time to address our personal needs and at a minimum, at least administer first aid.

It's been five weeks since Deb found the lump. I am going with her to the appointment to hear about how they plan to treat her. Unfortunately, so is Russell, her asshole husband. From the day Deb called me to tell me she found the lump in her breast to the day we went for her first appointment with the oncologist, the lump grew a lot.

How much? It was the size of a tiny little pea, and now it is the size of a lime. Our grandmother suffered from the effects of breast cancer and the subsequent treatment. Grandma was miserable from the chemo. She was diagnosed and treated in the '70s with surgery. Then in the late '80s, it returned, and she had a mastectomy, chemo, and radiation.

Grandma was always concerned about everyone else. As soon as one Christmas was over, she would start making small purchases for the next one. Most of the time, it was from Avon or the dime store. She never forgot anyone. We all received presents from Grandma. She even would give her mailman and neighbors a little something. Deb is a lot like Grandma in this way.

Grandma moved from New Mexico to Kosciusko, Mississippi. My aunt and uncle live there, and Grandma wanted to live out the rest of her life close to them. Visiting Kosciusko is like going back in time, with its quaint shops and old-fashioned hospitality.

Mom and I made a trip to Jackson when Grandma was sick. At times, I laid in the hospital bed with her while Mom drove around Jackson, trying to find her latest "craving." When I was a little girl, I loved to sleep with her, so it felt natural to crawl up into her hospital bed. Grandma craved all sorts of foods, but when Mom brought them back to her, she could only eat one or two bites due to the blisters in her mouth. I think Mom must have visited a dozen or more restaurants in those few days.

As I sat painting Grandma's toenails in her hospital room, I could not figure out why it smelled so bad. She and I both were clean, but the place stunk. The trash was empty, and the room looked clean, too. Finally, while standing outside in the hallway in front of the room, I stopped to ask her nurse about the odor.

She pulled me away from the door and told me it was the smell of death — an early sign that Grandma's organs were starting to fail.

Mom and I flew back home, and Grandma died a few weeks after that trip to Jackson.

C HAPTER 8 – YOU WILL BEAT THIS

"Deb, you *will* beat this. You know it's going to be okay . . . right?"

Russell has been an ass all morning. He challenges everything that is said. He is even rude to the receptionist. I hate him. Why is he even here? I am asked to wait outside while they talk with the doctor. They let *him* in and not me! I occasionally have issues with my cell phone, so luckily for me, there are still pay phones in use, although they are disappearing.

I am on the phone with my mom. "Mom, why are you crying? We do not even have a prognosis yet."

"Denine . . . is there a Denine out here?" someone asks.

"I am Denine," I reply and then say into the phone, "Mom, I've got to go; they are calling me back."

The healthcare provider guides me. "Can you come with me, ma'am?"

As soon as I walk into the room, I see Deb's face. I see asshole Russell's face. The doctor reaches out his hand to shake mine, and I am forced to take a seat. I want to run out of there, but I give in and act like I am strong and like I might for a minute be okay. I am the middle child. I can do this. Deb will rely on me, and she will survive this awfulness. It already looks awful, and I am not sure really what *it* is.

"Your sister has Stage 2B breast cancer, and we will have a better understanding after we have the results from the other tests. I understand your family has experience dealing with breast cancer previously; your grandmother died from it, correct? We have discussed the options and feel it is in Deb's best interest to start chemo tomorrow."

I'm wondering why he is so casual with my sister. Why is he calling his new patient Deb? He doesn't even know her. Her name is Debbie.

"We plan to reduce the tumor before removing her breast."

WTF? I want to scream, but I can't. Remove her breast! Jesus, already!

Deb looks right at me while the doctor asks, "Denine, do you have any questions?"

"Do I have questions? Uh, yes, a few."

He also asks me if I have any concerns.

Concerns? "Yeah, I have a few of those, too. Can we please start over, and may I ask why she will start chemo tomorrow? That seems urgent to me."

The doctor tells us, "It is a fast-growing tumor. We do not have all of the answers yet, but we feel our first course of treatment is to start her on chemo immediately."

I am unable to think clearly. So much for planning to take control and asking all the right questions. I'm speechless and wondering if I ordered enough blueberries for tomorrow's event, and if Carlos had washed the ton of dirty Romaine that I left by the vegetable washstand. Russell will be useless.

He is an asshole who will not help one bit! I no longer can hold back my tears. I sob like a baby. Deb is crying, too, and we are left wondering how this will work out.

We have a party for 300 in the morning. I should be at work, but here I am. I need to be here with my sister. She cannot do this alone. How will I tell Mom? Will I let Deb tell her? I can't breathe. I feel like I am going to choke. I feel hopeless and scared to death. I soon realize this is just the beginning.

Deb is not stable now, nor has she ever been. She is an alcoholic who smokes a pack or more a day. Do I tell her to stop smoking and never to have a drink again?

As we leave the hospital, she and I instinctively reach for each other's hand. We continue walking out while holding hands just like we did when we were little girls -straggling be-hind our mother toward the interstate as Mom led the way to our new life in New Mexico. There is a vulnerability that is suffocating us both.

How do we tell the girls? How do I tell Bailey that her aunt is sick? Caleb will be okay because he is a boy, and these days, he only knows girls and baseball. Meaghan has already experi-enced how hard life can be. She loves her mom more than life itself.

How will she survive this? What can we do to ease her pain? Ana has come to love Deb, too, and she considers Deb, her mom. She also has suffered much in her young life; so how will she deal with Deb's sickness and another letdown? Will they feel like this is just one more blow in their life? We have learned one thing for sure. Life is unfair. We came in separate cars, so we each make our way back to home and work. Deb wants *me* to tell Mom. Of course, she does!

So, it begins.

As I walk into the kitchen, Mom screams at me, "Where have you been, Denine? Why has it taken so long?"

I am pissed and start screaming right back and blurt out that Deb will start chemo tomorrow and has Stage 2B breast cancer. Mom is shocked and breaks down, sobbing and sobbing over the tiny desk in the front of the kitchen. Our employees are looking at us as if we have finally gone bat shit crazy. We have!

As I ponder the mess we are in, I look around at my sur-roundings. This is the place I spend so much time in every day. Our kitchen is small but very efficient. When you first walk into the kitchen, you see a small desk and computer area full of cookbooks, notes, vendor invoices, and menus. Some refriger-ators and freezers share the tiny space. Then you walk through an opening into the real kitchen where shiny, stainless-steel prep tables line the middle of the area. A large, commercial stove with 15 burners and ovens, both regular and convection, take up the end and left side corner. The dishwasher and racks run parallel with the prep tables on the other side. It's all convenient. At the end, closest to the front door, is a large, fat, stainless steel, four-shelf rack that holds tons of food items, spices, foil, and commercial-sized clear wrap.

Many hours later, I finally get home, and Jake tries unsuccessfully to console me. I am too worked up. He's irritated, so he slams the door as he walks out. I am holding on by a thread.

Jake is protective of me. He does not want me to go to work tomorrow and wants me to sleep in and take it easy. He does not understand why I feel the pull to be there for everyone else. "That is impossible," I tell him. "Deb is sick, and I have responsibilities." No doubt, we will battle over this mess for quite some time.

Would Jake notice or even care if I punched a hole in the wall? I want to hit something, anything, everything—even him at times! Several hours later, he finally comes back home, and I am sound asleep.

In the morning, Jake wakes me up with a hot cup of coffee. He started this tradition soon after we were married. I love him for trying to console me and for the morning coffee. We sit on the bed, discussing what will happen next when he asks me about my breasts.

"I have never felt anything strange."

"But do you do self-breast exams?"

I respond quickly with, "I am fine, Jake."

He gets agitated and jumps up to leave for work. We kiss goodbye, and that is that.

I reach for the phone to call Deb when she walks into our bedroom. "I just passed Jake; everything okay?"

"Yes, we are fine."

I ask her what she is doing here. I can tell she is eager to find out what Mom had to say about her diagnosis. "Did you talk to the girls yet?"

"Yes, but how is Mom doing?"

"Deb, Mom is okay, but she's upset. We are here for you, but we are all upset. How are the girls?"

"They are upset but doing okay for now."

"So, when is your appointment?"

"At 1:00 p.m. Are you coming with me?"

"I can't, not today, but I will be at all of the other ones; I am very sorry, but we have that party today."

"Denine, I will be okay, and I know you have to work, so don't worry about going to any of the other appointments, either."

"Deb, I will be at as many appointments as I can; if I can't, then Mom will be."

Bailey runs in when she hears Auntie Deb's voice. She jumps up and gives her a big hug. I fight back the tears when I see Deb tearing up. Bailey asks her why she is sad, and Deb tells her she loves her so much that it makes her cry happy tears. Deb leaves to meet up with Russell for the appointment. I have a bad feeling about that. I do not think Russell is up for this. He is a delicate little piece of shit of a man.

Several weeks have passed. Mom and or I have gone to all of Deb's other appointments. We are going again today to meet with the team of doctors to discuss the next step. More chemo? Is she done? Does she have to have surgery? Today is just Deb, Mom, and me. We have been together through so much — this is how it should be. Deb is feeling the effects of the chemo, so I drive her and Mom as far up to the front door as possible. Mom goes in and grabs a wheelchair. After parking the car, I run up the stairs and hope I won't get lost in the hospital. I do not want to miss any part of the appointment. I need to hear every single word that comes out of the doctor's mouth. A doctor whom I've never met speaks to us about Deb's initial results.

The news is not good.

"Your sister has Stage 3 cancer, and the plan is to operate in four days." Between her last appointment and this one, I did my research. Stage 3 implied she had a 5-year survival rate of like 49% - 56%. She will have a complete mastectomy. The chemo has done its job and shrunk the initial tumor, but cancer has spread to her lymph nodes. She will be admitted to the hospital today. We need to remain positive.

I resolve; she will beat this. In the catering world, we always round up, so this will be no different. Her survival rate is 100%, *not* 56%!

I blurt out that she is not prepared to stay. We did not even pack an overnight bag. "Are you aware that she has two daughters at home?" I ask. "Her not coming back home today will freak them out. Is there a reason you could not have warned us before this appointment?"

They remain scary calm and proceed to tell me this is not my cancer and ask me to hold all my questions to the end. Meanwhile, Mom is stunned and silent, and tears roll down her cheeks. They tell me they are aware that I have been there for my sister from the beginning. Their goal is to work with her and help her through this process, and they need me to support them so they can do their job. Bullshit. She is *my* sister! Deb speaks up and says she will do whatever is required.

How can I help Meaghan, Ana, and Bailey when I do not even know what to do myself? I do not want to leave Deb. Several hours pass, and the girls are at home with us. Deb's surgery is tomorrow. We plan to arrive a couple of hours early to allow everyone their time with her. They are not little girls, but they need us. They need our support and love. In the meantime, I will take care of the business, so Mom doesn't have to leave the hospital.

Murphy's Law strikes again. Suddenly, we are inundated with new business, looking ahead at a full calendar for the next six months. How in the hell will this work? How will we manage our time?

Jake is taking our kids and Deb's girls for pizza, which I appreciate so much. The kids are close to Jake and will listen to him. He is smart, and he will help them understand about the surgery. He knows how to stay calm; he may be the only one. Their absence will allow me to get through the pile of paperwork and unpaid invoices. Since Deb's diagnosis, we have not been able to stay on top of it. We are drowning in paperwork.

Deb makes it through the surgery and is resting peacefully. We are all breathing a sigh of relief, and the girls are laughing and planning what they will do when she comes home from the hospital. If feels good to laugh again. Mom had her housekeeper go clean Deb's house from top to bottom. Jason purchased plants and flowers for Deb's pots, and Jake mowed and trimmed her yard.

In our family, we all share another sickness -- we love gardening and planting flowers. It's an obsession. On the first visit to the nursery every spring, what starts out as a "quick" trip just buying a couple of plants to improve our outdoor scenery quickly turns into more than we can handle. It eats our lunch every time. Deb has not been able to plant anything this year, so Mom is making sure that when she gets home, it's all done!

Dumb old Russell graces us with his presence for all of five minutes in the hospital after Deb is out of surgery. He says he doesn't like hospitals. Like the rest of us do?!? Asshole. Men are weak, or should I say *this* man is weak? I can't stand him and cannot figure out why he is incapable of just sucking it up.

The doctor who put me in my place earlier in the process has just left. She is brilliant! I like her now. I feel Deb is in good hands. She said Deb did very well in the surgery, and they are waiting for the pathology report to come back, but she is hopeful.

Our master plan is for Mom to stay at the hospital and for me to run the business until Deb is released. We have completed four parties this week, and I am missing Mom's help. I am running on a couple of hours of sleep and would love to crawl into bed with Deb.

Caleb has a break at school, so he is home for a week. He offers to help, so he will spend time with us at the kitchen washing dishes; our usual dishwasher decided this was the best time for him to leave New Mexico. No notice, no nothing. He just left.

Finally, I get to the hospital. I am looking forward to hanging out with Deb — just the two of us. I get there in time to hear the doctor tell us how sick Deb is. The cancer is very aggressive, and Deb will have to continue the chemo, and will also have radiation. They will insert a port in her chest for easy chemo access.

I am so sad about the updated prognosis. I cannot imagine how my sister must be feeling. At this very moment, I am wondering how we will get through the next few months. We cannot cancel any of the events.

We were not planning on lousy news today. What just happened? Not only is it our livelihood, but we have several employees who rely on us. Our clients are lovely people, and they would understand if we canceled, but that is not how it works.

A couple of hours have passed, and Deb is sleeping soundly. I insist that Mom go home for the night. I will stay, and if anything changes through the night, I will call her. Jason and Cindy walk Mom out to her car, and it is just Deb and me. She wakes up. I think she was pretending to be asleep anyway. We laugh about it. That night, Deb and I talked about everything we ever did to piss Mom off. We share stories about our sex lives, like how often, positions, and the big question: Hairy or shaved? If you have a sister, perhaps you've had similar conversations. After many hours of gut-wrenching laughter, we both fell asleep — for real.

Mom and I helped Meaghan and Ana plan a "Welcome Home, Mom!" party for Deb when she was released. Russell brought Deb home, and we were all at the house, eagerly awaiting her arrival. It was like welcoming a new baby. Our excitement was infectious. The only thing missing was the silly baby games!

We were laughing and having fun. It felt like old times. Good times. We were altogether without a care in the world. The house was spotless, and the flowers in full bloom. We timed it perfectly; so, when they arrived, Deb could enjoy that "just-mowed grass smell."

C HAPTER 9 – LOWRIDER AND TORTILLA CHIPS

Everyone is working like crazy in the kitchen. We have 60 additional servers due to the high numbers this week. Our client is from the Dallas area, and *their* client is the Hispano Chamber of Commerce. The event we are catering is celebrating a Chicano traveling art show. Cheech Marin of "Cheech and Chong" fame is also displaying his personal art and is the MC of the event. The theme is organic southwestern cuisine and decor. For fun and to stay with the theme, we borrowed a "low rider" El Camino to serve iced cold sodas out of the back.

A lowrider is a customized car originated by Mexican-Americans in Southern California. Many lowriders have hydraulic suspension systems (modified suspension) so that their rider can change height at the flip of a switch. Lowriders are commonly classic cars from the 1950s. Albuquerque is full of them!

Coincidentally, we crossed paths with Mr. Marin (Cheech) years earlier in Roswell. He and Tommy Chong chartered a flight from Roswell to El Paso. When Dad returned from the trip, he bitched about it for years because they trashed our brand-new Cessna. They paid for the damage, but that was not the point.

We plan to fill the back of the lowrider with ice and Jarritos, which are Mexican sodas with real fruit flavoring. That's just for starters. We will also set up several food stations throughout the venue. We are making and serving a variety of salsas, quesadillas, pinwheels, stuffed red potatoes, corn, green Chile tamales, and blue-corn tortilla chips. We are using small, outdoor chimineas to display the chips.

Jason came up with the idea to set galvanized tubs on mini brick walls to hide the Sterno from the guests and keep the tamales hot! It looks very organic, and it's something unique.

As Mom answers and hands over the phone to me, I can feel in my stomach that it's my sister calling. Although I am extremely busy with work, I still remember to think about Deb. It has not been easy for her. After all, this is her cancer and her life. Since she got sick, she has not been able to work or "volunteer" in the kitchen at all.

"Hi, Deb," I say.

"Denine, can you come over tomorrow and meet with the nurse and me?"

"At your house?" I ask.

"Yes."

"What time?"

"Noonish."

"Sure, no problem, Deb. What is going on? Why do I need to meet her?"

"I need you to help me clean out my port; it is infected, and we will need to do this twice a day until it is cleared up."

Gulp gulp. I can't do this. Shit. Maybe Deb will figure out that I am the worst possible person for this job. I do not want to do this, and I know I will vomit all over her if I get near that opening in her body!

Accidentally aloud, I say, "Ugh!"

"Denine, do you not want to? I know you are very busy this week," she whimpers on the other end of the line.

"Deb, it's not a problem; I only said 'ugh' because I feel bad about it. I feel bad for you."

"Okay, I will see you tomorrow, thanks."

"Deb, I love you."

"I love you too, Denine."

I tell Mom that I am leaving soon. I have been in the kitchen since seven this morning, and we have a long day tomorrow. She asks me about Deb and tells me she sounded a little "strange" on the phone last night.

"Mom, Deb is going to be fine."

Jake and the kids are waiting to eat dinner until I get home, but all I want to do is get home and take a bath, followed by bed. To eat with them will mean another conversation about our messed-up lives.

I feel guilty because I have not been there for my family in months. I know I am neglecting Jake and am going through the motions again. To my joy, the house is spotless, and the smell coming from the kitchen is mouthwatering. Soon we engage in conversation about how I am failing at our marriage and our life together.

Jake sternly tells me, "You should try to spend more time at home, Denine."

I had several glasses of wine in me and did not hold back my anger. I said shitty stuff that I wish I could take back. My husband loves me and forgives me, but I cannot excuse my own bad behavior! I am a bitch. Thankfully, tomorrow is a new day, and I always try to start with a prayer and a positive outlook.

The nurse is pulling up to Deb's just as I do, so I introduce myself outside by the crooked sidewalk in front of her home. She seems like a genuinely compassionate and sweet person. We go inside. Deb is sitting at the kitchen table, waiting for us. We wash up, and the nurse begins to remove the bandages from Deb's port. I am standing there, in my usual form, making stupid small talk - which I hate to do!

That is, at least, until I see IT. I SEE THE HUGE, GAPING HOLE. On a person her size, it looks about the size of a dessert plate. I get weak in the knees and tell them I need to sit down. Deb laughs. The nurse reassures me that it is not the most significant hole she has ever seen. She says it's infected, and we must get it under control immediately, or Deb will be back in the hospital.

They are talking, but I am numb and for some reason, do not hear a word they say. Instead, I am thinking about those damn tamales that we need to finish making. The nurse looks at Deb and asks her how much alcohol she has been drinking and in what combination with the prescriptions. I come back to earth when I hear that and am no longer distracted by the tamales, or work at all.

"How much alcohol . . . what?!? Deb, are you drinking again?" I ask.

"Not very much, but I am angry. I am fucking pissed off." She snaps.

"By the way, where is everyone? Is Meaghan at school, and where is Russell?"

Deb starts talking, telling both of us that she has hit the wall and feels like giving up. She cannot do more than she is doing now and that her low-life, piece of a shit husband left her. He walked out and left all of them. I am flabbergasted. I ask Deb if Mom knows about this. She says no.

"Do the girls know he is gone?"

"Yes! Why are you asking so many questions, Denine?"

"Deb, I am worried, worried sick at this point. How come you didn't tell me before today? Or tell Mom?"

"You and Mom are always busy, Denine."

Deb continues to tell the nurse and me that her life is terrible. The utilities are close to being disconnected for non-payment, and Russell quit paying the mortgage two months ago. I walk into the kitchen to look in the fridge, which is almost empty other than the vodka in the freezer. The nurse is taking an inventory of Deb's pills.

She starts asking Deb about them. It appears she has been over-medicating. That, with the drinking, is a recipe for disaster. The nurse seems to be worried. I go into the other room and place a call to Mom.

Mom arrives a short time later, and now the four of us are discussing the situation. Mom and Deb are arguing. The nurse is trying to reach someone on the phone. I tell Mom about the utilities, mortgage, and even worse – there is little food in the house. Mom assures Deb that she will take care of everything and not to concern herself with the fact that Russell, that son of a bitch, left them high and dry.

Mom will get things paid and will continue paying every-thing until Deb is back on her feet. Then she pushes the issue. "Deb, what are you thinking, mixing alcohol and pills and no food in the house for you and Meaghan?"

Deb calmly says, "Fuck you both. Get out of my house!" She screams at us to go back to our "perfect lives."

"Deb, are you kidding?" I snap. I tell her that my life has completely done a 180, and I am close to not having a life; not one that I recognize, anyway.

"Deb, I have dropped everything to help you, and Jake is always mad at me because I am always gone, and when I am home, I am checked out. I feel like I am always putting fires out. Jake says that I do not put enough work into our life together and that when I am home, I do everything down and dirty, as fast as possible, to be able to check it off. So, if that is the 'perfect life' you are referring to, then I guess I should get back to it."

The nurse steps in and calms the situation. Meaghan is home now, too. Mom heads back to the kitchen because she needs to, but also because she knows I will be able to calm Deb down faster if she leaves, and we can get the port cleaned out. The process of cleaning the port makes me nauseous. I am hold-ing back the vomit and my tears all at once. I cannot let on to Deb how much cleaning her port sickens me. I must try to get peace back in her life no matter how hard it will be on me.

The nurse reassures me that I can do it. Twice a day is mandatory. Preferably at 8:00 a.m. and 8:00 p.m., so basically, in 12-hour increments. After seeing the panic in my face, she assures me that we have a little wiggle room with the 12-hour timing thing and that I do not have to change it until tomorrow morning. Oh, gosh, shoot me now.

Two hours later, I am on the road headed back to work. I am cranky, tired, and utterly pissed off. How did we get here? What happened? Will Jake divorce me and find a younger, calmer woman that does *not* have a family? How can we get Deb back? She cannot give up! *We* cannot give up!

Back at the kitchen, we worked another seven hours or so,

and when I finally left, it was 10:00 p.m. I must sleep, shower, and be back at Deb's by 8:00 a.m. Then work a 15-hour day tomorrow. Oh, and carve out at least an hour at 8:00 p.m. to run to Deb's and then back to the kitchen. I do not know how I will survive this one!

I am back in the same situation that I was in when D was born -- Jason's first kid. My clothes reek from all the foodstuffs from the kitchen, including more salmon. I am on the freeway headed home. It is very windy outside, and my car is not maintaining the road very well. My exhausted soul needs to get home. I crank up my stereo to try to give me a nudge of energy when I see it. Red lights in my rear-view mirror. 'Are you fucking kidding me right now?' I'm getting pulled over!

Yep! Oh, Jesus, this is the last thing I need!

Once my car stopped, I dropped my head down on the steering wheel and placed my hands at the 10 and 2 positions. My gesture was anything but gentle. All I wanted to do was cry.

"Ma'am, do you know why I pulled you over?"

"Nope."

"You were swerving all over the road. Have you been drinking tonight?"

"Nope."

"Can I have your driver's license, registration, and proof of insurance?" A few minutes later, I scream out, "Here is my license and registration; I can't find my insurance card. But I have insurance." A thought flickers through my mind. 'How did my life get so disorganized.' Great, now where is my insurance card?

"Officer, give me a minute."

"Ma'am, can you please step out of the car?"

"Why?"

"Ma'am, please step out of the car."

"Shit."

"What did you say?"

"I said 'shit,' and I am not drunk. I am irritated that you stopped me. So, there it is; shit, shit, shit. I am fairly certain you cannot arrest me for cussing."

He has me walk the line. He instructs me to lift a leg while holding a finger on my nose. You know, all the stuff they make drunk drivers do. Due to my exhaustion, stress, and the fact that the wind was blowing 80 miles an hour, I failed the "field sobriety" test.

We wait and wait and wait.

What a colossal waste of time. The officer is confident that I am drunk and advises me to cool it. All I want to do is get back into my car and drive as fast as I can. Flee the scene of this foolishness. Can I do that? How long would it take for me to bond out of jail? Would Jake bring the money to get me out? Or, as I fear, would he leave me there to rot since I have been such a bitch to him? And who in this family could clean out Deb's port if I am in jail?

Lately, Jake and I are at odds; we want our lives back. Before Deb got sick, we were busy, but not like this. We were happy; we were in love. Life was good.

Finally, a female officer arrives to escort me to the police van with the breathalyzer test, which is about five miles away. Once inside, they administer the breathalyzer test, which I PASS. Once I am cleared, the original officer that stopped me, apologizes before driving me back to my car.

He appears to feel sorry for me as my sobs continue, tears flooding my cheeks. I try wiping them with my shirt, but it stinks so bad it sickens me. He tells me he is going to follow me home to make sure I get there without further incident. Luckily for me, the truck driver had not towed my car away yet!

When I got home, to my relief, Jake was sleeping. There was no way in hell that I was going to wake him up to tell him what had just happened. No one would believe my crazy life! Even I don't recognize it.

By the time I showered and crawled into bed, I had to concentrate hard to control my trembling body. I was traumatized. Silently I cried myself to sleep.

I awaken to Jake, handing me my morning cup of coffee. "Good morning, honey, how did it go last night at work?"

"Fine, we got a lot done, and we are a little further than we thought we would be. I need to run a few errands this morning after I go to Deb's, and then I will start on the flower Serape rugs that I told you about."

The flower Serape rug is a decor idea that Mom and I came up with when we first started planning the chamber event. We had Jason go to the feed store to get us chicken wire, which was cut about five feet long. We have started painstakingly filling every tiny pocket with a wildflower.

We are using hearty summer flowers in many colors. These are varieties we never use in catering, but they work great for this project.

To prepare it, first we bent by hand and folded the entire piece of chicken wire to resemble the folds of a rug or blanket. It's somewhat wavy and random. Once all flowers are attached, it will make for a beautiful centerpiece. It's two days and counting until the chamber event, and everyone is in good spirits.

It's about 7:30 p.m., and it's been a long day at work. Just as I am about to leave to go to Deb's to clean out her port, she walks into the kitchen. I am in shock. We all are. To my knowledge, she has not driven since she first got sick. Rene is here this week to help, too. Although she knows what has been going on with Deb, when she sees her, she is startled.

We are all standing at a prep table in the kitchen, and I am looking at Mom for answers -- reassurance that we are not going down that rabbit hole again. Mom is looking at me for the same reassurance. Okay, great, now what? We do not have time for this, but I guess we are dealing with it anyway.

Deb knows everyone in the kitchen, so they chat and catch up with each other. Finally, as timers chirp in the background, everyone gets back to work.

"Did you bring the stuff for me to clean out your port?" I ask.

"No."

"How come, what's going on? You seem a little off."

"Do I?"

"Deb, yes, you seem off. What is going on? Have you been drinking?"

"So, what if I have ... what the fuck business is it of yours?"

"That's what you have to say to me, Deb? Let me guess; it's the first thing to come to your mind, right? I cannot talk with you when you are drunk, Deb. I just can't. Not tonight."

Mom is visibly upset and is not sure what to do. She again looks at me for answers.

I snap, "Mom, why are you looking at me?"

You can feel the tension and panic is starting to set in for all of us. If Deb is willing to drive here drunk and be open about it, she is spiraling out of control. What could have happened if she had been pulled over by the police? Geez, I cannot imagine that fiasco!

"Who can we call?" I ask. I always think we can call someone for help, and they will magically appear. However, that doesn't happen unless *I* am the one getting the call.

Deb did not lose her hair immediately when her chemo started. They weren't even sure she would. We knew it could happen, but I promise you, we were not prepared.

Let me explain my thoughts on this a little better in order to not sound like a heartless bitch. If it were not for the drugs and alcohol, seeing my sisters' bald head would not even matter to us. Her bald head is not the issue. We love her unconditionally no matter what she looks like. But the gloom hanging over us is crippling. We dream of her survival and want her healthy, but seeing her out of control while using drugs and alcohol is making those around her sick. Our hearts ache for her to be well.

Chemo is supposed to help you. Losing your hair can be a side effect of the treatment. So, under normal circumstances, although losing your hair is traumatic, it is part of the recovery. A person's mental health is crucial and losing your hair can affect your psychological well being. Hope is huge when dealing with cancer. It is a journey that takes time. Our family understands this very well. In our case; in our family - we were not prepared to see her like this.

I frequently hear people say it is liberating or beautiful. On occasion, I hear about groups of people that will shave their heads - a huge gesture of support for a loved one. In our presence tonight - I see no beauty; only horrific pain.

Earlier, when Deb came in tonight, she was wearing a scarf. We had not seen her in a scarf before. Someone in the kitchen tells Deb that her scarf is lovely. I think to myself, "Lovely? What's lovely about it? You're an idiot."

To our shock and great sadness, she rips off the scarf and blurts out, "See this, it's gone. My fucking hair is gone. I have lost everything."

No doubt, losing her hair-triggered her drinking and over-medicating tonight. I can hardly move, but I feel like I need to run. I want my legs to work, but I am frozen, and my knees are locked. What is wrong with my legs?!?

Finally, I break free of my own body and head back to the restroom, but shit, Deb follows me. I hear her mouthing off to Mom and can feel her closing in on me; I feel like if I stop to turn around, she will bump right into me, which I would not want to do at this point. That would scare me to death!

In the back of the kitchen, after taking one step up to a landing, there is a restroom to the left and one to the right. We keep uniforms and tablecloths hanging between the restrooms. I ran into the one on the right and quickly close the door. In retrospect, I wish like hell we had put locks on those doors' years ago! As she barges in, I am mad, furious, in fact.

Again, I cannot help but wonder how in the world we arrived here. I'd love to punch her in the face. Knock her out cold. I am so over all of this crap!

On her way in, she grabbed a hanger and began hitting me with it. At first, I nervously laughed at her until I realized she was serious - In shock, and uncertain who was crazier at that moment, Deb, or me.

She was screaming, crying, and cussing AT ME, all at the same time. She was more upset than I have ever seen her in our entire lifetime. I was getting cuts, gouges, and scrapes all over my arms, neck, and back. They stung, but not as much as the pain I felt in my heart, which was *breaking*.

I felt desperately sorry for my sister. At one point, she scraped my face with the edge of the sharp hanger, which was dangerously close to one of my eyes. I felt the cold and wet blood running down my flushed cheeks. With no other choice, somehow, I found myself on the floor behind the door as Deb continued wailing on me with the wire hanger. She was hysterical; and had lost all control.

Mom and Rene are shouting out, but they stand frozen in place, presumably as I did a few minutes ago. I get it — they are paralyzed too. As I cower down further behind the door with my arms stretched out over my head, I pray I awaken from this fucking nightmare. Thank God, she got the hanger stuck in my hair. *Those are words I never thought would come out of my mouth!*

Baby chunks of flesh mixed with blood and hair are on the floor around me. I am traumatized and seriously freaked out. A few seconds later, the screaming, jabs, and hair-pulling stop. With a smirk on her face, she looks down at me. She tells me how sorry she is and how funny I look with a hanger stuck in my hair. To my shock and surprise, she smirks; sort of like a faint laugh.

Again, frozen in place. Crying, and the deep pain and tears are thick in my throat. I felt that if I did not sit up straight or get up, I would literally choke to death. I had that lump in my throat, and it was blocking my airway. I needed to get to my feet, but that was easier said than done. I was stuck behind the door, and the area is cramped. Salty tears burn the wounds as they pour down my face.

As I look up, Deb says, "Why are you still on the floor, Denine, do you plan on getting up anytime soon?"

In addition to every other feeling that is piercing all my nerve endings, I needed to pee. If I move, I will surely lose it. Deb knows that about me, too. Even our employees know that I run in and out of the restroom all day. If I have been out at an event or shopping, they know I will run in and head straight to the bathroom before I do anything else.

Deb sneers at me, "You have to pee, don't you?"

"Yes, can you help me up?"

I reach up my hand, and she gently pulls me up with ease as if we had been playing a game this whole time. Just as I make it to my feet, the pee starts to flow. I know I will pee my pants if I try to move. So, I hold myself, legs crossed, firmly holding onto my damp crotch. I do not move — not even an inch.

Deb is laughing, and now I am starting to, as well. What else can I do? I let go; the warm urine is flowing down my leg and into my shoes; I am at a loss to stop it or leap to the toilet for one last "save." I don't have it in me any longer.

Soaked in pee, I take all my clothes off to change. We have a tiny little chest of drawers in the restroom that is full of panties, panty liners, etc. We also have extra one-size-fits-all chef pants hanging up with the other uniforms, next to the other empty hangers. I grab a pair of pants and *all* remaining hangers. I roll up the hangers in my dirty wet clothes for disposal later.

Deb is making fun of my panties. She said they look like the "day of the week" panties she and I used to wear when we were kids. We are both laughing. I try to exercise that middle child personality thing to keep her calm until we can make our way out of this hell. Whoever said, "When you're going through hell, just keep driving" had the right idea.

Again, I am ill-equipped to know what Deb is capable of doing next. I do not even know who she is at this moment. Complete forgiveness rushes over me. I look in the mirror, and I do not recognize my reflection. I do not even know who *I am* now. My face seems destroyed due to the blood smears, but all I can think about is what just happened. I genuinely felt like it was an "out-of-body experience."

Deb moves closer and is standing right behind me at the little sink. So close, I can smell her. As we look at ourselves and each other, we both know this is a turning point. The depth of our sisterly sadness is debilitating.

Mom and Rene are finally brave enough to join us. We all stand in the bathroom, crying and laughing at the same time. To be clear, only Deb and I were laughing. Deb apologizes over and over. And all I can say to her is, "It's fine, you have earned the right to be pissed."

We all remember the scene where Joan Crawford beats her daughter after finding a wire hanger in her closet. To this day, I can see her face, all shiny from her night cream, with her hair pulled back and whacked-out crazy eyes. Deb had those eyes tonight.

To break the ice, I ask Deb if she has seen' Mommie Dearest' recently.

Straight-faced, she retorts, "No, but maybe we can try to watch it soon."

At that point, we cannot stop laughing. The irony of it. Nervous, ugly laughter. But our mother isn't laughing. Mom is visibly shaken and looking at the blood on my arms, face, and neck. She starts to help clean me up.

"I am fine, Mom, really, I am, and I will take care of it later."

Now she is irritated with me. Somehow, I need to make her understand I don't need or want to be <u>touched</u>. I do not want to hurt her feelings, but I have had enough touching for one night.

Still trembling and trying to control her crying, she gives Deb and me a hug as she leaves. At the door, she tells us she loves us very much and that she wishes it was her with breast cancer, not her daughter.

I drive Deb home, make her eat, clean out her port, and she and I go to sleep in her bed. We did not end up searching for the Mommie Dearest movie. I finally got a good night's sleep.

Physically, I was not hurt very much, but the emotional trauma remains. I will never forget that day. Never.

CHAPTER 10 – BEYOND BORDERS

The big event is over and behind us now. I was caught off guard earlier when Jake informed me that we were scheduled to go to our friend's house tonight for a birthday celebration. I promised several months ago to bring the cake. Why can't I seem to learn the word no?

Why did I agree to this? Oh yeah, I remember now. Because I *used to* have a life, and because Carolyn is my dear friend, whom I love. I love her, and I told them I would bring the cake. I call the kitchen to see if, by chance, miracles still exist.

"Hey, Carlos, can you please ask Kaye if she has an Amaretto Sour Cream Cake in the fridge? Tell her it is for Denine."

Mom gets on the phone. "Why do you need a cake? You are coming in today, right?"

"Yes! I will be in soon, but I forgot about Carolyn's birthday, and the party is tonight."

"Did you forget that you promised to take Meaghan shopping to look for a new dress?"

Shit.

"What did you say?"

"You heard me, Mom, don't pretend like you didn't."

"Denine, what has gotten into you lately?"

"Jesus Christ, I just can't imagine what it could be, Mom."

WTF, she hung up on me . . . Again! What is wrong with us?!? I call back.

"Mom, why did you hang up on me?"

"Because of your mouth."

"Wow, so that's your solution, Mom, to hang up on me?"

Okay, good for you.

"Denine, I am just as stressed out as you, and I would appreciate you not cussing so much."

An hour or so later, I arrive at the kitchen, and I am irritated. I have just busted my ass working on one of the hardest events of the year while dealing with my sister, her cancer, and the insane schedule causing our lives to spiral out of control. I think Mom could cut me some slack for the day.

I know she is hurting, and I know she is frustrated; we all are. But I am not the enemy here. I am sick to death of getting treated like shit. I feel like I have eaten enough crap to last a lifetime.

Meaghan is not ready to go to the mall yet, so I will work on billing and paying bills until she is ready. As it turns out, there are small miracles amid trauma. We *do* have an extra cake in the fridge and Mom offers to decorate it for me. That is her way of saying sorry. God forbid she utter the words "I am sorry!"

Carolyn will be happy, and I am not letting another person down. I realize I desperately need to getaway. Mom does, too. But when and how is the question? Neither of us can leave until Deb is out of the woods.

After a few weeks, I have finally mastered the art of cleaning out the port in my sister's chest. I no longer get grossed out; it's somewhat routine now.

While bathing Bailey, I notice a mark on her hip. Her tiny little hip. After calling the doctor, I am a little concerned but will keep it to myself. Why stress anyone else out? We will take Bailey in on Thursday to have it checked out. I have noticed it before, but it was not as big. It has gotten larger and changed in appearance over the past weeks.

Thursday comes, and we make our way to the appointment. Meaghan is with us, too. She and Bailey are close, and I am glad she was able to rearrange her schedule. Finally, Toni, our family doctor, comes into our room. As we chat back and forth, Toni asks me if I am nervous. I explain what our family has been going through lately, and so yes, I am stressed about this.

She says, "Well, let's take a peek."

I am studying her face, as I have grown accustomed to bad news and feel that if I somehow know before she utters even one word, then I will have enough time to digest the bad news or celebrate the good news. But Toni's face is silent. She does not reveal one damned thing.

I blurt out, "What do you think it is?"

Meaghan looks at me and says, "Tia, it's okay."

Meaghan is right, and after all, look at what this child has been through with her mom. She is right.

Toni starts to speak, "It looks suspicious, Denine."

"What does 'suspicious' mean? What are we going to do? Is it cancer, Toni?"

"Denine, you have to stop talking, and you need to listen to me."

"Easy for you to say, she's not your daughter!"

"No, but she is my patient, and I *am* her doctor."

Bailey cannot be sick! Fuck! We cannot go through this with this child. My child! Our family cannot suffer more heart-ache. Just as I am silently planning how I will care for Bailey *and* Deb; Toni abruptly interrupts my reverie. She says we should cut it out today.

"What! Today? Jesus! Why today, and why the hurry?"

"Denine, when I said it looks 'suspicious,' what did you think that meant?"

"Okay, I get it, sorry."

Nurses start coming in and out; Bailey is given a mild oral sedative to calm her. I am feeling weak in the knees. I want a sedative, too! Why am I not stronger, and why do I get so crazy? I should call someone, but I can't think of anyone. My family is already dealing with too much. We have been with the doctor a while now, and I know Mom will soon be wondering why we haven't called or stopped by the kitchen.

Meaghan and I eventually lost track of exactly how many shots and stitches Bailey endured. Toni had to cut much more extensive in order to get clean borders – more than she anticipated.

At one point, she says, "I think this was a little too much for an office procedure; I probably should have referred you to someone else."

Toni tells me it looks like melanoma, but we cannot be sure until pathology is back. Before I can react, Bailey starts to cry. My focus turns to her instead of how I am feeling. The part that is cut out is in an area of Bailey's body that is always covered up. How can it be melanoma? I do not understand it.

Toni is explaining, but I have zoned out. All I hear is that it could be deadly. Bailey was a trooper, but she is wincing and crying a little. She could not have gotten through such a hard day without her cousin Meaghan.

We are on our way, and we have prescriptions to fill, so I take the girls to the kitchen. We have a small one-person cot that we can set up in the kitchen. Bailey is groggy, so she should sleep while I run to the pharmacy.

When we pull up near the front door, Mom is literally standing at the door. She looks pissed.

When Meaghan sees Mom, she whispers to me, "Here we go, Tia."

Mom begins, "What in the world? Why has it taken you so long?"

"Why is Bailey asleep?"

"Mom, stop!" I snap. "They cut it out today because it looked suspicious."

"Oh my God, Denine."

Meaghan begins speaking, "Meems, she has a bunch of stitches and is sleepy from the medicine. Tia has to go to the pharmacy, so I'll watch Bailey until she gets back."

I need to get home with Bailey, but I still need to clean out Deb's port. How do I do both? We live clear across town, but Deb lives only a few minutes from here, so I need to go now and do it early to work it into my insane schedule. I have no choice today. Hopefully, cleaning it out a couple of hours early will not hurt anything.

CHAPTER 11 – RUN AS FAST AS YOU CAN

Bailey's screams tear me out of deep sleep; I run into her room. She appears, okay. I do not see blood, and she is cool to the touch, so it's not a fever. Toni told us to watch for these two signs.

"Mommy, I had a bad dream."

"Honey, it's okay! Everything will be okay, I promise."

"Am I going to die?" she asks.

"No, Bailey, you are not going to die anytime soon. You are going to be okay now, and you have a beautiful future ahead of you. We are all going to be okay, even Aunt Deb."

"Mommy, if I tell you something, will you get mad at me?"

"Bailey, I could never be mad at you. You can tell me or ask me anything you want."

"Aunt Deb is going to die. We were holding hands in my dream, so does that mean I am dying, too?"

"Bailey, Aunt Deb is very sick. That is why we pray for her every day, but she is not going to die anytime soon."

Here we are again at the "Holy cow!" crossroads of life. My daughter may or may not have melanoma, and my sister has advanced breast cancer. Could life get any harder?

While taking a shower yesterday, I felt a lump in *my* left breast. Do I also have cancer? If I say anything to ANYONE, the bells, whistles, and alarms will never be silenced. I will make an appointment with Toni, but for now, I will tell no one. Not even Jake.

After a short day at work, I arrive at home. Jake is on the phone and seems aggravated. Soon I realize his aggravation is with me!

"Why are you looking at me?" he blurts out.

In return, I ask him if he is okay and if there is anything I can do.

"Now, you want to help, Denine. Now, you have time for me. For all of us?" he says.

"Yes, Jake, I want to help. What can I do?"

"For starters, you can spend more time here than dealing with your fucked-up family and working all of the time. I never see you, so if we are going to live single lives, then I am out of here."

"Are you kidding me, Jake? Really. You are hitting me with this when you know what has been going on? Fuck you, Jake."

"You bitch. I'm out of here."

He doesn't get it, and I wish he would feel the suffering like we do. Maybe then he would understand that not everything is "arms and legs." For the overall good of the family, shortcuts are essential. Down and dirty. That's my style.

His own family is pretty screwed up, too. And in some ways, even more so than mine. Jake has never understood how hard it is when someone you genuinely love is sick or dies. He still has his parents, grandparents, and two siblings. He has yet to learn his family's dark secret about his younger, biological sister who was adopted out at birth.

In anger, he blurts out words like, "I don't give a shit about their life or what is happening in the news. It's not our life, and it's not our concern."

I am confused by this type of thinking, but then again, I'm the one who does the charity stuff. I donate clothes, furniture, household items – not Jake. Luckily for me, I am not really attached to much. Sentimental items yes, but I don't give any other material items a second thought. I have been this way my entire life and Jake doesn't understand it.. or me for that matter.

I'm the one who stops to give a buck or two to the guy standing at the intersection holding up a sign. I do not think for one moment that my one dollar is going to change that person's life, but I think if you have the nerve to stand out on the street begging for money, then who am I to question what he or she does with it? Although it is more comfortable for me to look away, I resolve to be a better human. I know the person standing at the corner belonged somewhere, once upon a time. *He was someone's son, and she was someone's daughter.* I purposely make eye contact. I hope that for a moment, they do not feel judged. I want to ask them to come with me, but I know that it is an illogical solution.

Thank goodness, Bailey is sound asleep, and Aubrey and Nicole are at Jake's ex-wife's house. I am going to try to get a better night's sleep myself. I decide to go up to the deck with my bottle of wine in tow. For miles, all I can see are stars. I begin to regret what I said to Jake. He is my husband. How could I talk to him like that? What is wrong with me? I try calling him, but there is no answer.

Of course, he will not answer his phone. He is crying out to me to pay more attention to him, and all I do is take on more. Will he forgive me? Can I forgive myself? Will I now have a divorce to deal with, too? I do need to put him first. He is a good guy. He strikes out at me when he is angry. Deep down inside, he worries about me. I know that.

Here I go again — Middle child syndrome. I am making excuses and allowances for his bad behavior. His anger comes from the way he was raised. He had a childhood drenched in problems caused by well-meaning adults in charge of his care, using drugs and alcohol.

Then came the abandonment, poverty, and hunger, never knowing for sure when and where the next meal would come. He has had intense emotional crises from abandonment issues. Even though Jake has a lifetime of bad memories, he tries not to let them control him. He is a kind man and a kind human.

As I reach over to answer the phone in Jake's absence, I realize I am not getting coffee in bed this morning. Immediately, my first thought is "Oh shit'!" Given my life, I assume the worst every time the doorbell or phone rings. So many thoughts – all jumbled up in my twisted head.

"Hi, sis," is what I hear on the other end of the line.

"Matt, is that you?"

"Yes, I just called to say I love you and was thinking about you, Mom, and Deb."

"How are you, honey?" I ask.

"I am good, just wishing I could be there to help with Deb and help you and Mom."

"You should be out soon, right, how much longer?"

"Not sure, maybe a few months."

From the sound of his voice, he is fighting back the tears. I wonder if he also gets that lump in his throat as I do. He tells me that he received a long and heartfelt letter from Deb and that she sounds positive. He said he is sending her and me a poem along with a hand-painted handkerchief. The writing and drawing are art therapy, and it is helping him. He no longer thinks his life is completely over, but instead, he has a reason to go on. He has hope. With great emphasis, I tell him he better not go anywhere, and he needs to get out and get on with his life here with us.

"We cannot have anything happen to you too, Matt. And it would probably kill Mom."

The annoying beep of the call ending in a few seconds signals us to say our goodbyes.

"I love you, honey."

"I love you too, sis and tell Mom, Deb, and the kids I send my love."

When our garage door opens, it makes a pretty loud whining noise, which signals that either Jake is home or there is an intruder. I stand quietly in the kitchen, waiting. It is taking a long time for the door from the garage into the kitchen to open. It is Jake, and it startles me.

Why it surprised me is a mystery. I knew someone was in the garage. It is apparent that I am jumpy and on edge. I do not want to be kind. I want to scream at him, but I stop when I notice the look on his face. He looks like a kid that lost his best friend.

Jake tells me he is very sorry, and he will try to be more understanding. At this point, the fight is out of us. We stand there in the kitchen, hugging each other for a few minutes. We start talking about everything that has happened up to this point.

As if he is reading my mind, Jake tells me that he does not know what it is like to lose someone close to you, and he ponders the thought of how he will handle it when the day comes. So, the *real* reason he has been irritated with me lately why we just had this huge argument begins to reveal itself.

"Hon, have you seen a doctor yourself?"

Of course, I say no. "Why are you asking me that?"

"You know why. You have a lump in your left breast. If I can feel it, I am sure you can as well."

"How long have you known?" I ask.

"Denine, the question to be answered is, how long have you known?"

"I just felt it myself a couple of days ago, and I have an appointment with Toni in two weeks."

"Are you an idiot, Denine?"

"Wow, here we go again, Jake. Thank you for your deep understanding."

"I did not mean to say that, hon. I am the idiot, not you. I love you and cannot imagine my life without you. Considering what Deb is going through, I think you should try to get in sooner if you can. That is all, I mean."

After a while, the conversation gets a little lighter. Jake wants a motorcycle and has been window shopping. I encourage him to get it. I have no reservations about it and think it would help him feel better about his life. Riding can be liberating, and as far as I can tell, he is a safe driver. Additionally, it would be a great outlet as well as a distraction from our issues— from our shitty life! We decide to plan a day together to go look at the bikes.

CHAPTER 12 – WHEN THE PLANT DIES

We have a pretty light week on the schedule, so I am taking a couple of days off to recharge my mind and soul. Additionally, now I only need to clean out Deb's port three times a week, so I am off the hook for another day. Jake and I are going out on a date, which will start with a light dinner at our favorite restaurant.

It's easy; requires little thinking on my part. We love going there because they know us well. It is comfortable and familiar. I always start with a glass of Ménage à Trois, a mellow blend red wine that I love, and Jake will have either a Long Island Iced Tea or beer.

After our last big fight, we have both agreed to try to understand each other better. Jake is compassionate about what the family is going through regarding Deb, and he finally realizes that I must continue doing my part to help. His only request is that I make time for us. Tonight, is not just about a date or sex. It is about reconnecting and spending time together, especially since we have been living like roommates due to my life. I remember why I fell in love with this wonderful man. He is a great guy, and I am hoping he will remember why he loves me!

On our way home, I realize I had missed calls from Mom.

"Mom, you called. What's up?"

"It's Dad."

All Jake could hear was a long sigh coming from me. I look at him and shake my head. He is trying to figure out who I am talking to and asks if it is one of the kids.

"No, it's Mom; Dad is in the hospital."

He doesn't react. Why should he? After checking in on

Bailey, I leave for the hospital. Thirty minutes later, I walk into Dad's room just in time. He is covered in blood. He has an issue at times now with bleeding too much. After having a heart valve replaced several years ago, he is on Coumadin for the rest of his life. The Coumadin has caused a lot of bleeding problems that are difficult to resolve permanently. Dad begins to tell me that he may get to go home tomorrow if all the tests come back okay.

"That's great news, Dad! Excellent news! How did this one get started, and how did you get to the hospital?"

He begins to tell me that he was sitting at the kitchen table when the blood started pouring from his nose. He laughs, reminding me of his theory on a plant that was given to him when he had the transplant years before.

"When that plant dies, I will too." He further states, matter-of-factly, "I have a great family, and I have been blessed to travel all over the world and have had a pretty good run. I do not have any regrets. I'm ready to go at any time now; I have seen enough of this life."

Just then, my eyes gaze over to his bedside table, but I immediately decided that was the wrong thing to do as my stomach does a flip-flop. Covering the table are blood-soaked gauze bandages that were used to soak up his blood. It's the same table used to receive his food tray. It repulses me. I've seen too much. Body fluids. Blood. Mucus. Chemo. Needles. Tubes. Urine. Feces.

It makes me nauseous. I can't even eat in the hospital cafeteria even though I know the quality is excellent. The lines are getting blurred.

The last time I took Dad to the E.R., we used a 1# sour cream container to catch the blood. We save the containers for food that we are giving away. Dad loves the shrimp and avocado salsa, which is why he had the sour cream container at his house.

There's not a moment of peace. Mom is now calling me, too. Jesus Christ – I already need another break!

"Denine, do you have time to run by the kitchen when you leave the hospital?"

Ugh!

"Have you spoken with Matt lately?"

"Yes, Mom, a couple of days ago."

"Did you know he has a friend that he wants us to hire?"

"Yes, he said something about it."

"What are your thoughts?" she asks.

"Mom, can I call you when I leave the hospital?"

"Okay."

I assure Dad that either Jason or I will be there to pick him up in the morning. Dad and Mom separated a few years ago. She would gladly go and get him, but it is awkward between them, so Jason, Cindy, Meaghan, and I juggle the responsibility. Dad is easy, and it is never an issue.

My issues are only about finding the time in my hectic schedule. I am pretty sure Jason is picking him up this time because I have Bailey's follow-up appointment about the possible melanoma. My phone rings again, and it is Mom. *Shocker*.

"Denine, I thought you were going to call me when you left the hospital."

"Mom, I am just now leaving. My phone may die because I am still in the parking garage, and there is bad reception in here."

"Why are you still there?"

"There was an issue which turned out to be a false alarm, of sorts."

"Is he okay?"

"Is who okay? Dad?"

"Yes, Denine, Dad. Who else do you think I would be talking about?"

"Oh my gosh, yes, he is fine, Mom. I, on the other hand, am losing it. What is up?"

"Did you talk with Matt about hiring his friend?"

"His friend, you mean. His prison roommate. Yes, he told me a little about him."

"What do you think?"

"Mom, as little as possible at the moment. I am exhausted and trying *not* to think. You should be tired as well. I know you've had a long day too."

"I am, but I am sitting at my computer designing a menu for the big event at the winery. Matt probably will call one of us tomorrow, so whoever talks to him needs to tell him to have his friend stop by the kitchen when he gets released from prison."

"Mom, due to his prison record, I think we will need more than a yellow sticky for this one. I will pick up employment applications early so he can fill one out. We actually should have a file for new applicants."

It has been a couple of weeks since Prison Nick started working here in the kitchen. He seems like a good guy so far. We did not share the information that he is a convict with our other employees, but he did. Mom and I are having coffee while working in the office on new menus when Matt calls to see how it's going with Nick. I ask Matt why Nick went to prison. Matt shares that Nick and a restaurant owner got into an argument, and during the discussion, he locked up his boss in the walk-in freezer. Luckily for all concerned, his boss did not die, but he was mad as hell when he thawed out.

Nick also tells us that he was addicted to oxycodone at the time, which is why they did not give him more prison time. Instead, the Judge demanded he is sentenced to a drug clinic for treatment.

"Wow, Matt. So, do you think he could be a danger to us?"

"Mom picked him up the other day because he did not have a ride into work, but based on what you just told us, I don't think she will be doing that again."

Mom and I are laughing about the crazy things we have gotten ourselves involved with and agree that until one of us is chopped up into pieces and thrown into the freezer, Nick can continue working here. It feels good to laugh like this. We also ponder the possibility of Nick going off on one of our employees, Sue because she can be irritating. Sue has worked for our family in one capacity or another for about 16 years now.

She used to take care of my brothers when they were younger. Like Carlos, you can count on Sue. The thing about Sue is this. At times, she lives in a fairytale world, fantasizing about getting married, which she has never been, nor has she had a boyfriend. Nick is cute, and they seem to get along well. So that makes me a little nervous.

I love Sue and do not want to see her get hurt. We can pretty much guess what she is going to say, based on the girly way she has been acting. For now, we are content with the fact that they are working hard, and there have been no issues. Let's hope it stays that way.

C HAPTER 13 – BLOODY BUBBLE BATH

While waiting to hear our name called, Bailey is fidgeting, and I am growing impatient. We usually get right in when we come to this medical center, but today is not going as planned. Finally, we are called back, and there is the usual small chit chat banter back and forth. We go past the scale and nurse's station until we end up in the very last room at the end of the corridor. Does that mean we will be the last one seen today? Bailey and I are both restless. The knock on the door signals us that Toni is here and ready to come in.

"Bailey, how are you feeling?" She asks.

"I'm good."

Toni asks Bailey if she wants to go down the hall to play in the elephant room so she can talk with me. At that, Bailey jumps off my lap and follows the nurse back down the long hallway.

After she leaves the room, I blurt out, "What the F is wrong?"

"The biopsy is positive for melanoma.

I cannot breathe, and I am agonizing over what I need to do next. How can this be happening to us? What in the hell did we ever do to God to deserve so much pain? Why are we being tested over and over? I have always thought we were good people, but apparently not.

Fuck the universe; I am done with my lessons! In a dizzy state, it feels like my chest will crack wide open and catapult my heart across the room. Just slam my bloody organ against the wall. What would happen, then? Would I be dead?

As Toni continues talking, I hear nothing. I can only think about how in the hell we will survive this. How will Bailey deal with this? She assures me that she did get clean borders when she removed the tumor, but since the biopsy is a positive melanoma, the recommendation is to hospitalize Bailey for a day or two. That way, they can run tests and perform another minor surgical procedure, which will ensure clean borders. I am still pondering the word "tumor," which was an epic failure on my part as I missed every other word Toni said, so I ask her to repeat what she just said.

"Denine, are you okay?"

"Yes, I am fine, but my daughter, sister, and father are not."

She scolds me and tells me that my only concern at this time should be for Bailey. She is very young, and this type of melanoma is not common. We need to proceed aggressively and not leave one stone unturned. Deep breathing comes in handy when you feel your throat is going to close itself off.

I am finally grasping the situation and do not want to continue talking with Toni. I trust and respect her very much and feel we need to take a day or so to adjust to the news as well as to clear my schedule.

Bailey is my main priority. Deb has been holding her own lately. Dad has lived a beautiful life, and although I love him and am very concerned, I also know his fate is out of my hands, and Jason will be there for him. Bailey and I leave with a handful of information. I thank them, and for a split second, the lump in my throat gets in the way as my "thank you" comes out.

They must have known Bailey has cancer because they could not have shown more compassion to us. Our next stop is McDonald's. We finished our Happy Meals and hit the road again. While driving home, I am rehearsing in my head what I will say to the family. Mom is the one I am most worried about, then Deb.

Mom's timing, as usual, is impeccable. Bailey fell asleep as soon as I put her in her car seat. I call out her name to ensure she is asleep before answering the phone. It's Mom. "Denine, do you have the results yet?"

I begin uncontrollable desperate crying.

Mom orders me to come to the kitchen so we can talk. I hang up and try to gather my emotions and thoughts so that I do not scare Bailey if she wakes up. Just then, out of nowhere, I slam my fist into the dashboard. I want to break my hand. I need to feel something other than the pain from so much sickness.

Upon arriving at the kitchen, we are greeted by sad faces as well as happy ones because Bailey doesn't go to the kitchen very often, so our employees love it when she does. They spoil her rotten with hugs, kisses, and candy. Although she is unaware of her diagnosis at this point, she is acting weird. Her intuition is strong.

She asks Mom, "Mimi, why are you sad? Did you hurt your feelings?"

We sort of laugh at the way she phrases the question. Mom assures her she is fine but sad because she did not get to see her for a couple of days. "But now I am happy because you are here, Bailey."

Mom said that Carlos has been in the walk-in for the past hour, rearranging it, so it's probably time that he came out.

"Bailey, can you go see if Carlos is ready to come in out of the cold? He will be happy to see you, honey."

She runs off to find him, which gives us a chance to discuss the devastating news.

"How bad is it?"

"She has melanoma, and the biggest surprise to me is how rare it is."

"Rare?"

"Yes, the doctor said melanoma in someone Bailey's age is rare. She gave percentages that were like two to four percent, which would make it rare."

"Why or how do you think she got it, did they mention that?"

"No."

Mom's face, so familiar to me, now looks like mine when I get bad news. It isn't so much the look as it is a deep sadness. Mom begins sobbing. I want to take her pain away, but I am unable to move. The realization of the diagnosis is paralyzing. If Mom is reacting to the news like this, how will everyone else feel? How is Bailey going to understand this?

Bailey's world revolves around wearing her pink tutu and playing dress-up with her dolls; she will no doubt relate her cancer to her Aunt Debbie's.

I plan to go to the bookstore to see what books are available for children diagnosed with cancer. I know we need to be positive. Bailey notices how we frequently laugh even when times are stressful.

"Mom, I know we will figure it all out, and her doctor is confident Bailey will get through this and be cancer-free. We should hear from the doctor's office tomorrow. They must make the arrangements first so that it runs much smoother for Bailey. She will be admitted into the hospital for a couple of days and will undergo surgery in the same area that Toni worked on. It seems pretty technical, but I know they will take great care of her."

"Does Deb know?" Mom asks.

"No, not yet. You are the first one that I told, and that's only because you called me, and the second I heard your voice, I broke down. I am very sorry, Mom. I did not mean to."

"You never have to worry about that, Denine. I know you are going through a lot. Too much, in fact. We all are Mom; 'just a little too much reality for a Saturday night, huh!'

I am going to talk with Deb; even before I speak with Jake or Chris. I do not want her to hear it from anyone else. She is going to flip out, and I need to keep her calm. She will not be able to go to the hospital due to her weak immune system, so hopefully, we can minimize the news and keep the part about the hospital stay and surgery away from her.

"Mom, can you watch Bailey for a couple of hours so I can run some errands?"

I plan on calling Caleb in a day or so to let him know what is going on, but I want to have more information available before I do that. I think I will see if Chris wants to meet Jake and me for a drink, and I will tell them both at the same time. For now, I need to get to Deb's to tell her.

A few minutes later, as I am pulling up to Deb's house, I call her. She doesn't answer her phone, so I use the key that she had given me a few months back to unlock the front door. Suddenly, I have butterflies in my stomach. I get them very quickly these days. My internal compass. The house is tranquil, which is odd. Deb always has music on, usually something from the '80s, or even disco. I call out her name, and thankfully, I hear a response. *Thank God*, now I can breathe again.

"Denine, I am in the bathroom. Come in here."

"Deb, I will wait out here for you."

"No, Denine, I need you to come in here, please."

There it is. I knew today was turning to shit. Why would she need me in the bathroom if everything is okay? I slowly open the door and begin walking in, but I feel the frozen leg syndrome thing. My body does not want to move.

Is she holding a hanger again?

Once inside, I notice the bathtub is almost overflowing. Deb is skootched way down, so only her head is above the water. Is she soaking in bloody bubbles? I had to think about that one. Was that blood or pink bubble bath? Jesus – what is wrong with my thought process?!

I feel that sickish feeling. You know the one you get after you see something you're not supposed to see, and you kind of already know the outcome.

"Deb, tell me that is pink bubble bath and not blood, I beg!"

Our eyes meet, and her silence indicates to me that, in fact, it is a bloody bubble bath. Oh my God, when will this nightmare end! I now know not to expect more in this life. I set myself up for failure by waking up daily with a hopeful outlook.

I came here to tell her about Bailey, but apparently, this is not the time. I reach for a towel and tell her we need to get to the hospital. She remains calm while I lose what is left of my damn mind.

As we drive to the hospital, which can take a good 30 minutes, I am wondering about the reality of our lives. We are crashing. There will be no survivors. You can't make this shit up. Our lives are a mess.

The bubble baths I took with Jake where we would sit in the tub together, drinking wine, laughing, and enjoying each other are gone. Now I must figure out what I am supposed to tell Mom, and how we are going to tell Deb about Bailey.

After we get into the hospital, somehow, I need to figure out how I can slip out for a moment to make a couple of phone calls. Mom cannot bring Bailey to the hospital, so I need to reach Bailey's dad or Jake. Just then, Deb asks why Bailey isn't with me.

I tell her, "Mom wanted to spend time with her today."

"Bullshit. You are a liar, Denine. I know something is wrong. I can see it on your face. You don't have to protect me. I was in the kitchen earlier and thought I heard them talking about Bailey being sick. Is that true?"

"Yes, Bailey has cancer, but it is treatable and very different from what you are going through. Who took you to the kitchen – by the way?" I ask.

Deb immediately starts screaming while I am driving, and the words go straight through my head like a bullet. I know I need to drive faster and get her to the hospital. We are almost to the emergency exit when an ambulance comes flying past me and cuts me off. I am down to one last nerve, which is hanging precariously off my neck.

The sirens startled me like no other time in my life. I feel shaky, unnerved, and close to what I can only assume is a nervous breakdown.

Maybe we could get two hospital beds in one room for the price of one. Deb tells me she is okay to walk in on her own. So, after dropping her off, I made my way to the parking garage, where as luck would have it, there is a space immediately next to the elevator. Thank God! Finally, a break today.

CHAPTER 15 – SUPERHUMAN POWERS

A couple of days have passed since we brought Deb into the hospital, and I am now preparing to admit my daughter into the same hospital on a different floor. The excellent news will be that Deb and Bailey can visit with each other if they are both gowned and masked up. Jake was right, we should have canceled this week's events, but work must go on. Mom is exhausted from being at the hospital, but she will not leave.

While checking in and signing all the forms to admit Bailey, I am in a stupor. Mindless signing. My yearning for my sister and daughter to be well is so intense that it strips me of any other wish or desire to do anything. Anything at all! To me, life without either of them would be a devastating blow followed by grief that would suffocate me — never-ending!

My guilt for being healthy is also overwhelming. I may have a lump in my breast that turns out to be cancer, too, but even if it is, I know that I will survive. After all, they are only tits, and they can be cut off. Yes, my life is a mess. It is not the life I had planned.

We have an enamel bowl that sits on a table in our entryway at home. It reads, "I always wanted to be somebody . . . I see now I should have been more specific." I find myself thinking back to a better time.

As an example; before I married Jake and after I divorced Chris. I have never been a prude, nor have I been promiscuous, but I have dated quite a few people. Some briefly, others a little longer. And yes, sex was part of that, too. So was cooking together, eating together, movies, hiking. You know, all the usual stuff. I met several awesome men during this process.

Most days, I was happy, too. My kids were good; I was okay. Life was mundane yet beautiful. I counted my blessings and rarely remembered how my life was so disrupted when I was little and growing up.

So, as I prepare for what happens next, I need to wrap my mind around the blessings and the good in our lives.

My survival mechanism; a master compartmentalizer. If compartmentalizing was like a good cook, then I am the Masterchef of the family! As if holding my hand, daydreams lead me out of the misery. I am reiterating this to you in order to explain that it has not been what I strived for in life. Would I have preferred a better existence. Absolutely. I am a realist and in hindsight of several decades, I see it protected my heart. Allowing me to grow and mature. This character flaw is how I am able to sit here today counting my blessings.

Although Dad is not well, he is improving every day. Mom is my primary concern. She, like me, is healthy, but it is not her physical health that worries me. This time, she has not left the hospital even once. Moreover, we drink too much in this family. Deb is not the only alcoholic. It's a cycle we go through. Drink. Don't drink. Drink again. Our family is plagued with alcoholism. Today I regret my openness in drinking in front of my children. I made it look fun and cool; all the while my kids learned to soak up all the damage, dysfunction and abrupt chaos caused by my drinking. I cannot go back now. There are no do-overs in life; all I can do now is try to do better today.

Bailey does not seem interested in what is going on. She knows she is going to have an operation and a few tests, but she is not concerned right now. Her only agenda is when will she see Aunt Deb.

Yesterday went by quickly, and Bailey and I slept well throughout the night. They started some of the tests late yesterday, and she will have the surgery in the morning. Bailey is required to ride in a wheelchair to Deb's floor.

That thrills her, so we are off. Once we get to Deb's room on the other side of the hospital, I scold Bailey because she immediately wants to jump up and get in bed with Deb. She is always in one of our beds, and it is my fault for allowing it!

Deb scolds me. "I expected Bailey to crawl into my bed, Denine."

"Deb, you are sick. They do not want you that close to anyone."

"No, they do not want me close to her." She tells me she is not contagious, and that Bailey can lay there if she wants.

I never win when it comes to those two. After an hour or so, Deb tells me that she wants to go downstairs to get fresh air, which means she wants to go for a smoke.

"Do you think that is a good idea, Deb?"

"They told me it's a little late now to stop smoking and that I should try to stop once I get home."

About that time, Deb's nurse comes in. "Hi, beautiful," he says to her.

I can't recall his name until I heard Deb say it.

"Lance, tell my uptight sister it is okay for me to go smoke."

"It is fine as long as she stays in her wheelchair. Who is this little princess?"

"Lance, this is my niece Bailey. She is having an operation tomorrow."

Lance asks what type of operation. Briefly, I explain she has a rare melanoma.

Bailey asks, "What is a mellynooma?"

We chuckle, and it is Lance that explains to her what a mellynooma is. He tells her it is cancer but that in her case, she will be superhuman after she wakes up from her operation.

"Bailey, the doctors are going to put a little magic wand inside your leg that will make you big and strong."

Bailey asks him what color the wand will be.

Lance tells her, "It will be a rainbow of colors, and it will change colors every time you have to do a superhuman trick. Maybe orange when you do your chores and then perhaps it will be yellow when you go to the park to play. It will constantly be changing as you grow up."

Bailey asks if Aunt Deb will get a magic wand put inside her so she can be superhuman, too. Lance explains that Aunt Deb can't have an operation, so we will have to pray that she gets powerful by taking medicine and that the "big" machine is cleaning her blood, which will help make her stronger, too.

Why do nurses know precisely what and when to say something? Good nurses always do! And, how in the world did Lance have stickers in his pocket? Deb and I both assumed someone must have given him a heads up. Lance asks Bailey if she wants to choose a sticker.

After concentrating hard on the dozen or so stickers, she selects a Black Panther. She proceeds to ask Lance if she can have two.

"Of course," he says.

Bailey places one of the stickers on the big machine and gives the other one to Deb. "Mommy, Daddy told me that Panthers are strong, so now Aunt Debbie will get strong, too." At that, Bailey asks if we can go outside now to smoke.

Lance assures us that no one will mind. On our way to the elevator, I glance over at Deb, and she is snickering and making a gesture of "air" smoking. I get it. I can read her mind. We are laughing about the fact that my six-year-old asked if we could go smoke. There is an area out in front of the hospital near the side of the entrance, which is where we plan to go.

Once there, Deb lights up. I do not smoke, but I am offended by remarks and hateful looks coming from the folks that are passing by. They are harshly judging us. Bailey is in a hospital gown and wearing a mask. Lance told us the mask was to protect her from germs. Everyone is so judgmental.

I'm not stupid, and I am aware that it probably looks weird from their perspective. I never want my sister to feel alone, to be alone, or to think she is hated because she is sick and smoking. She looks sick. She knows "they" know she probably has cancer. And then what about that little girl? It is apparent that she is also ill! *There were stares*.

What will Bailey think if I smoke? Will she even remember me doing it? Ever since my sister's diagnosis, I have been walking through my life in a semi-zombie state. I look healthy on the outside, but on the inside, I am numb. Numb from the trauma that has been targeting us for months.

"What the hell, Deb, give me a cigarette." I say.

She laughs and tells me, "Denine, I see the stares. I don't care what people think, and you don't need to smoke to make your point with them."

I explain to her that I care and will not allow them to judge her! "Deb, I am the only person on this earth that can judge you. I love you, and they don't. Give me a damn cigarette already."

Bailey starts to giggle. She tells me that she is going to tell Jake about me smoking.

"Jake is going to put you in a time out, Mommy."

I light up, start laughing, and coughing. At that moment, our little family fit the mold for white trash dysfunction. And I didn't care! As a gesture of rebellion, Deb takes her knitted hat off, which reveals her bald head. There will be no mistaking why she is in the hospital now.

After smoking one cigarette, I am dizzy, but it was worth every drag. And I will do it again if I must. A while later, we made our way back up to her room to get her settled. In our absence, Mom was able to make phone calls. The minute we roll back into her room, Bailey blurts out to Mom that I was smoking.

"Bailey, you are a tattletale." I snap.

Mom gives me a strange look. It was her approval for my smoking. We tell each other goodbye, and Bailey and I make our way back to her room. That night there are four people; two parents and two children, all sleeping under one roof. Surreal. Sad.

The next morning and earlier than expected, two doctors and nurses enter the room. Bailey is sound asleep, and they are all standing there looking at us. I jump up quickly and put my hair up into a scrunchy. Just then, Mom and Deb roll in, and there are no words.

The doctors have no earthly idea who Deb is, but it is evident that she is a patient in the hospital. I make a quick introduction before Bailey starts to wake. She is startled by the activity and begins to wince. Deb excuses herself as she rolls past the line of doctors. *Deb is in charge.* Finally, she is at Bailey's bedside.

"Honey, it's Aunt Deb. Remember, today is the day you get your superpowers, so you have to wake up."

You could hear a pin drop in that room — total silence. Bailey starts to sit up, and unexpectedly, she is calm. She tells everyone hi. Again, in tattletale form, she tells them that I was smoking a cigarette last night with Aunt Deb. Jesus, Bailey!

I feel the judgmental stares and announce, "I am planning to quit soon."

With that, the process begins to prep her for surgery, and Deb and Mom go down the hall to a private waiting area.

Then, in single-file formation, first Chris appears, then Jake, then Dad. It has been an hour since Bailey went into surgery, and I am restless. My mind is swirling.

Although Chris needs to be here, I dread it. I do not like making small talk with anyone and speaking with him typically makes my blood boil. I am trying to think of something funny to say about the three stooges sitting here; each at a loss for words, but nothing comes to mind.

Then I remembered something I frequently heard from my aunts. Aunt Myra told me that Grandma Martinez did not have much use for men, and Auntie often reiterated that Grandma did not care for men and would say, "Men do not have the sense God gave geese." Another favorite of mine was Aunt Amee. Her real name is Margaret. She was very classy and I adored her. She also shared that same story with me, so I am certain it was a common thread in our family - about weak men. As I look around the room, these men are somewhat useless. Honestly, not always, but definitely today!

Have you ever smelled something that reminded you of an event from your past? I do; all the time. Smells and music are triggers for me. The area we were sitting in, smelled clean. Like when you walk into a Dry Cleaners. Fresh like that.

Out of the blue, I remember one reason my blood boils when I reflect on my marriage to Chris. It is a funny story – now, but at the time, his recklessness infuriated me.

After spending half a day cleaning out my closet and dresser -then sorting, I ended up with two large trash bags for donation. Easy enough, I thought.

A couple of days later, I called Chris to ask if he could drop off my work clothes to be dry cleaned. A few more days passed when I remembered I needed my two white tuxedo shirts and black pants for the weekend events.

Imagine my surprise when I was given the ticket and the total at the bottom read a whopping $316. I chuckled and stated I thought I had been given the wrong ticket. The clerk adamantly stated I owed it. At that I asked him how in the hell three items could add up to that much money.

He glanced over to the woman on the other side of the room. Presumably, his wife. She put her head down. I could tell she was *embarrassed* for me. They had my attention. 'What the hell' I thought to myself? The man says "Your husband left before I could ask him about the clothes. We wondered if there was a mistake, but I was unable to verify with him, so we cleaned everything."

In that moment I knew what had happened. If I could have run away without anyone noticing, I would have! In my horror, I knew this man – this stranger had seen my old panties and old stretched out bras. Also, old nightgowns, slips, ugly stretched out tops, pants, and even old shoes. Real ugly stuff; two large trash bags full to be exact!

I was furious and embarrassed beyond belief. I did not have $316 to use on cleaning; in fact, I only had $20 to my name! I did not cause this issue, yet I am the one that has to deal with it. Red face and all, I asked the kind man if I could pick through the pile to retrieve the three items I needed for work. "No ma'am, you must take all of it." Like I hadn't been embarrassed enough, I begged him to give me my three items. His voice was heavy and sharp tongued with an adamant, no!

Although I wanted to run away, I asked him as nicely as I could if he took *layaway.* He was silent. I was silent. His wife was silent.

I turned toward the door and left. A few minutes later as I was driving home, I knew I would never show my face there again. I left without paying or getting any of the clothes. While married to Chris, I was subjected to many embarrassing things; so much so that today, I rarely get embarrassed at all.

I chalk it up to life and lessons learned; Grandma Martinez was correct!

Back to reality as I gaze over at Deb, it makes me sad. And that lump in my throat is starting to cut off my air, so I stand up and walk down the hall. How are we to survive these issues?

Inside, holding on by that one little thread. How does my mom feel? How in the hell is she coping? I am worried sick about all of us. Just then, I look up and see Meaghan and Ana walking toward me. A sign of relief. They have tears in their eyes, too. We hug like we haven't seen each other in years. Chris walks out into the hallway and sees us hugging. He announces to Deb that the girls are here. Mom walks out to join us. She is worried sick about the girls, too.

Meaghan tells Mom that she can't shake the feeling that something terrible is going to happen and that she does not want to leave for camp because her mom is so sick. Mom tells her that Deb is going to be okay and that Bailey is not very sick, so she, too, will be okay. After a few more minutes, the oncologist finally comes in to update us on Bailey's condition. She tells us they had to cut out quite a bit more of the area to get clean borders, and that her lymph nodes were not affected.

"Bailey will make a full recovery; she is one lucky little girl, and I think you can take her home tomorrow."

Our waiting room is full of laughter and crying. For a moment, everyone is happy and getting along. No drama, no family issues. No fighting with one another. Hell, I was even pleasant to

Chris, and that *says* something! Deb announces she is tired and wants to go back to her room.

Chris and the girls leave to take her back over there. I tell her I will see her later because Chris is staying the night with Bailey. After a few more minutes, everyone disperses back to their regular routines. Whatever normal is.

Jake walks out with Dad. Earlier, they made plans to go to dinner, so I am pretty sure they will have a good night. The girls will be leaving soon, too, as they both have plans of their own, and we encourage it. Mom has finally agreed to go home for the night as I will stay with Deb. It has been another couple of hours now, and everyone is finally gone. I have my sister to myself. She is feeling melancholy by the way she is talking and acting as if she is dying.

"Deb, what is going on, and why are you talking like that?"

"I am tired, Denine."

"Deb, I know you are, but you have to hang in there just a little longer. We must let the medicine have time to work on you. So please promise me you will try -- you will try to hang on."

"I promise you that I will do my best, but we both know that usually is not enough, at least not in our family."

"Deb, do you know how much you are loved? We have spent our lives fighting, but you are my go-to person for everything. I love you so very much. You are, after all, my older and much wiser sister. Well, the older sister, for sure, Deb."

With that, Deb blurts out, "You bitch."

"I know," I say. "You wouldn't have it any other way."

C HAPTER 14 – AN ANGEL AMONGST US

Once inside, I ask Deb to stay seated while I go up to speak with the woman behind the glass window. She quickly agrees, and I am relieved she is remaining calm. I begin telling the woman that my sister needs to get admitted to the hospital as she is bleeding internally.

She almost snickers but stopped herself. "Are you a physician?" she asks.

"No, I am not.

"Can you have your sister come up to the window?"

"No, I cannot."

She is growing just as impatient as I am.

"Here is her insurance card and copay, can you please look at your records and start the process of getting her admitted quickly?"

"Ma'am, our policy is to take patients in the order that they arrive unless there is an emergency, then they move to the front of the line."

I blurt out, "No shit. This is not my first rodeo, lady; I have been here numerous times. The last time we were here, it was you that checked us in, and you were much nicer."

Suddenly, she gets pissy and turns her chair around to talk with her co-worker. Crybaby has feelings; who knew! She is no longer able to work with me due to my profanity, so she asked "him" to take over. With that, her co-worker takes the insurance card and the copay.

I wrote out the check for the copay since Deb left her purse at home, and even if she had it, there is no money in her checking account. Russell has not offered to pay one dime for anything, so Mom continues paying for it all. There is an issue with my check, so now there is a long delay in getting her admitted. Great!

"Ma'am, is the insurance in your name?"

"What? Are you kidding me? You are kidding, right! No, the insurance is not in my name; I am just paying her co-payment."

"So, you do not have a different insurance card?"

"NO!"

"Ma'am, there is an issue with the insurance, not with the copay."

"Oh, okay, well, what's the issue?"

"She is no longer covered."

"That is news to us. So that means her worthless, piece-of shit-husband canceled the coverage."

"Ma'am, if you continue to cuss at us, we will have to call security."

"Then call them! We have been here for over an hour, and you are just now trying to get her checked in, which frustrates me because she is very sick. To avoid any further confusion on my part, she does not have insurance. _**Sir**_, is that correct, and is that the current issue?"

"Yes, ma'am. Correct."

"My sister is hemorrhaging while we are discussing insurance. This is a county hospital, and I do not believe you can refuse treatment. I am begging you; please do whatever you need to do to get her admitted."

"I realize you are upset, but you need to calm down; we are here to help you."

"Then, please help. Is there someone other than you that can help resolve this issue? I do not mean to offend you, sir, but I am freaking out because my sister has been getting treated for breast cancer next door at the cancer hospital, and she is very sick."

After that, everything changed. The c-word is powerful! Who knew! A clerk comes out into the lobby to put a wristband on Deb and assures her she will be next. If you say the word can-cer or heart attack, it gets their attention. In the middle of all the drama from checking *her* in, I forgot to call Mom, or anyone, for that matter. I also turned my cell phone off because of the warnings posted all over the place. I tell Deb I am going to check on Bailey and will be right back. She asks me if I plan on telling Mom about the current situation.

"Do you want me to because I am not sure I can keep it a secret. Not today, anyway."

"Well, you were going to keep the fact that Bailey has can-cer a secret from me," Deb reminds me.

"No, I wasn't. The main reason I came to your house today was to tell you about her. That is the truth, Deb."

"Whatever, Denine."

I leave the room to make the call. "Mom, how is Bailey?" I ask.

"Fine, where are you?"

Does every single conversation have to start like this?

"What's wrong, Denine? I can hear it in your voice."

"Well, shit, I guess all of the women in our family are fuck-ing clairvoyants because you and Deb both have said the very same thing to me today!"

"Denine!!!"

"I went to talk with Deb and ended up having to take her to the hospital, and we are here now waiting to be seen by a doctor."

"For what? Do I need to come up?"

"It would probably be a good idea, Mom. Is Meaghan there now?"

"Yes."

"Mom, please ask her to watch Bailey. Make up any excuse you can. Don't tell her about her mom. I will call Jake and ask him to run by and pick them up. They can all eat dinner to-gether."

Sobbing begins again. Mom and I are both crying, and she asks me what happened. I let her know that now is not the time,

119

and we will chat about it when she gets up to the hospital. My lump is back in my throat, and I need to get it together before I call Jake, and before I go back into the hospital.

After five hours, Deb announces to me that she is ready to leave. She wants to be in her own home. I assure her that she will be called next; as I have already bugged the desk clerks a million times, and I know Deb is next in line. She *has* to be!

Again, someone with a fucking sprained ankle was taken back to a room before my sister. Maybe it was broke. I don't care. Who gives a shit; the bottom line - obviously, it is not a life-threatening injury!

It is times like this that our life is like psychological waterboarding -- a brutal form of water torture where water is poured over a cloth covering your face. You feel paralyzed as you are drowning – over and over again. The pain would be ex-cruciating. Although we are not actually suffocated by water, life has a way of rendering us hopeless at times. We logically understand that we will not die from the pain, but we still must experience it. The torture is brutal and paralyzing at times.

Deb had a hysterectomy years ago after being diagnosed with early-stage ovarian cancer, so there's no doubt the bleed-ing is not coming from her missing uterus.

As if an angel fell from the sky, I see my sister's cancer doctor walking across the hallway. I run after her, yelling back to Deb that I will be right back. The look on Deb's face when I return arm-in-arm with her doctor is priceless. In the brief seconds walking back across the lobby, I tell her what has hap-pened and that we have been waiting in the lobby for over five hours.

Deb is whisked off in a wheelchair, not by an orderly or another asshole clerk, but by the angel doctor herself. She walked into the triage area, grabbed a wheelchair, and that was that. Someone was trying to talk with her, but she kept push-ing Deb further away from that area. We end up at the end of a hallway.

The doctor tells us she will be right back, saying, "I need

to find a bed for Deb."

We chuckled about the "bed for Deb." It almost rhymes. Moments later, Deb is in a makeshift room. Although the E.R. is busy, the doctor wants to get the ball rolling, even if it means a temporary place. We are finally out of the lobby, and treatment can begin. An E.R. Tech comes in and very politely asks Deb if she can walk.

I blurt out, "Of course, she can walk."

She asks her to pee in the cup so they can start running tests. Deb scolds me with her eyes, so I back off. I inform the tech that it will not be possible for her to do that as she is bleeding.

The tech ignores my statement and instructs her as follows, "Ma'am, please get me a urine sample. Please follow the instructions on the wall regarding a clean catch."

"Deb, you heard her, go in and get that urine sample for the tech, okay!"

Deb and I are laughing because we know there will only be blood in that cup, and it will prove our point about internal bleeding. The tech finally returns to collect the urine sample.

She looks startled, picks up the bottle, and without hesitation, leaves the room. No words exchanged. That is a terrible way to drive a point home, and I would give anything if that had not been our reality, but it was, and all we can do now is wait. Suddenly, the concern for my sister seems to be the priority.

Several doctors rush into the makeshift room and discuss the plan to move her to another area. Possibly ICU. Mom finally arrives, too. She asks about Deb and is alarmed at the attention she is receiving. I assure her I will fill her in shortly and that everything is under control. Deb asks her how Bailey is doing.

"She said to tell you she loves you to the moon and back."

Deb doesn't say a word; the only sign of emotion are the tears running down her cheek. Once again, Mom and I must have seen her tears at the same time, because we both turn our heads away at the *exact* same time. During the past few months, I have seen Deb like this several times, where she quietly sits and cries. Quiet tears.

Several more hours have passed, and we agree I should get home to Bailey. I feel like a total loser leaving my sister and mother at the hospital. It is spooky leaving at night; long hallways, empty elevator, and a deserted first floor. Finally, I am in the safety of my locked car. It only takes me twenty minutes to get home. As I pull into the garage, I notice the clock in my car reads 2:11 am. Now, I am even a little spooked in my own garage. I assume it is because it is the middle of the night, and I am exhausted.

No one is up, and Bailey is sound asleep. I take a shower and fall asleep in her bed. In the morning, I am awakened by Jake, bringing me a cup of coffee, and asking me how my sister is.

In a low whisper, I tell him, "Let's get out of here. I do not want to wake Bailey."

Once we are in the kitchen, which is literally on the other side of the house, I explain everything I know and tell him how sorry I am that I was not home yesterday or last night.

He asks me about Bailey's appointment.

"Oh, my God."

For a moment, it felt like a million days ago when we met with her doctor. I cannot believe how I forgot about it. What the hell is wrong with me? I begin telling him about her diagnosis and treatment. I break down. I cannot hold back the tears, or the total despair I am feeling. It is a cycle of sadness and suffering. I almost feel like I am not human; existing in someone else's life. *This cannot be my life.*

After a few minutes of holding each other and Jake reassuring me that our marriage and our life is okay, I regain control of my senses, and we begin the lengthy discussion of Bailey's prognosis as well as how the next few days will play out.

He thinks we should close the business for a week or so. I assure him that our staff can manage the small events and that Mom will be able to run it from the hospital with phone calls. Some of the events have been on the calendar for months; we cannot cancel at the last minute. Jake reminds me that he can run interference and help wherever we need it. He has a ton of vacation time and will talk with his boss about the need to take time off right now. About that time, the phone rings.

Jake hands it to me and says, "Hon, it's Caleb."

Why is it when you need to be the strongest, you lose control of your emotions? The second I hear my son's voice, I start crying. Jake walks out of the room, I assume to give me privacy, but it is probably because I am crying, and he doesn't know how to help me right now.

"Mom, what is wrong? Why are you crying? Mom!"

"Caleb, I am fine."

"It doesn't sound like it. You are crying for a reason, so what is it?"

"That growth on Bailey's hip is cancer, and Aunt Deb went back into the hospital yesterday; she is bleeding internally."

Caleb asks me if there is anything else he needs to know, and I tell him that Grandpa is doing a little better this week, so that is a blessing.

"Mom, what is the plan with Bailey?"

"She will be admitted into the hospital this week, but only for a couple of days. They are planning on going back into that area to make sure there are no cancer cells left."

"Will she and Aunt Deb be at the same hospital?"

"You know what, Caleb; I am not sure. There is a children's cancer center on one of the upper floors of the hospital, but I don't know. So, what is going on with you, honey, and how is school?"

"Mom, I wanted you to know that I was nominated and am receiving an award, which is like a scholarship. It's an honorary thing based on team leadership, integrity, and sportsmanship."

"Wow, Caleb. I am so very proud of you. Is there a ceremony involved? Will I be able to be there if there is?"

"Why are you crying again, Mom?"

"Honey, I am emotional from all the stuff going on here, and I am so proud of you! I cannot wait to see you soon."

"Mom, are you going to be okay?"

"Yes, I am fine. I am stronger than anyone here."

"Tell Bailey I will call her after six tonight. Love you, Mom."

With that damn lump in my throat, I am barely able to get out, "I love you, too."

CHAPTER 16 – SNOWMAN AND S' MORES

Deb and Bailey are both out of the hospital and home. All is well in the world. I finally feel like our lives are headed in the right direction for the first time in a while. My anxiety has blossomed into hope. I am happy! After three weeks in the hospital, Deb was released with the understanding that she needs to be extra careful about everything. She cannot use too much energy, and she must eat better, and above all else, no alcohol!

We have many parties on the books and have been busy working on menus and schedules. Jake and I are thriving once again, too. He and I are happy with each other. Bailey's cancer scared us, but it was just that -- a scare. We are confident that it was just a blip in her life and that she will never have to worry about this again. Even though she will go in for regular testing for the next few years, I choose to stay positive about it. I am trying to put it out of my mind altogether!

Caleb will be home in two weeks for Christmas break, and we will spend our days laughing and cherishing one another. Once uneventful, now, any little activity is celebrated with enthusiasm and laughter.

We love every morsel of every single event we get to share as a family. Everyone seems excited about how things are right now, and we are counting our blessings even though I, too, have been hit again with another scare.

I had my fifth lumpectomy on my left breast. It was not cancer; the waiting on the results was agonizing. Hard on all of us. Due to my sister's ongoing breast cancer issue, I feel different this time. Mammogram and ultrasound. Always both tests.

Then comes the waiting on results. It is hard to stay positive and focused on healing after struggling over the past several months with Deb. I wonder if I will ever get my life back, or will cancer forever define me? Define us all?

After a lengthy discussion with Toni, I have made the decision that I will not go through this again. No more lumpectomies. No more waiting on results. If I have another scare with a "suspicious" lump, I will choose to have a prophylactic mastectomy. To date, every woman in my family that has passed away died from breast cancer.

I also must consider Jake's feelings. It is not the sexual part of breasts that worries me. It's the fact that I would no longer look the same. We are both relatively young, and it would be an adjustment. I guess I should also put this on the back burner. I may never need to "go there."

Jake is a good man. He is not at all like Russell, who left my sister shortly after her mastectomy because he said it "repulsed him." He is just a weak, pitiful little man. He disgusts me! I hate his guts.

Armed with good news from the doctor, we are going to the resort again for two days, which will recharge us. As soon as we get back home, our crazy catering schedule gets ramped up to warp speed. We have five or six events each day, every day for the entire month of December. In January, we will do our customary yearly shut down, and Carlos will be the only one working for about two weeks.

My morning starts with the usual cup of coffee brought to me by Jake. Bailey and I are lying in bed, wondering if it is going to snow today as our local weatherman promised during the morning forecast. While in the shower, I hear Bailey's shrill of a scream. I stand in the shower frozen, waiting for what is to come next.

She barges into our bathroom, "Mommy, it's snowing, it's snowing!"

It is what we wanted, but her scream takes me back to an earlier time when that was a usual pattern in our home. I breathe a sigh of relief. After hearing the forecast for continued snow, Bailey and Nicole run around the house collecting snow boots, socks, mittens, scarves, and those knitted beanies.

We play in the snow and our feeble attempt at making a snowman is coming to an end. It resembles an old refrigerator. Not round at all. There was not as much snow as we needed, so our snowman is full of dirt and twigs that stuck to it in our attempts to roll it. We are about to give up when Deb shows up.

Bailey and I stop what we are doing and run up to her car. Not giving her even a minute, we fling open her car door, and Bailey jumps on her lap.

"Bailey, get down," I say, but as usual, my words are ignored.

Deb tells us she is fine and has not felt this good in months. Bailey asks if she is still smoking. The smoking bothers Bailey for some reason.

"No, Aunt Deb is not smoking... at least not today, Bailey."

Deb reassures Bailey that she is trying very hard to quit, but she didn't get the special powers Bailey got when she was in the hospital. She asks Bailey if she can help her quit smoking by holding her hands.

Bailey starts to giggle and says, "Oh, Aunt Debbie, you are funny!"

About that time, Jake joins us and starts laughing his butt off.

"What is so funny?" I ask.

"Is that a snowman?"

"Yes, we are not done yet. Quit judging us. Do you think it is ugly?"

"Are you kidding?" At that, he starts to walk away.

I am baffled at his attitude, and just before I begin to yell at him, I see him enter the code into our garage keypad. The garage opens, and the next thing we see is a snowblower. He has never had an opportunity to use it. An old neighbor gave it to him before relocating to Destin, Florida. Jake tells Bailey to run and get Nicole and Aubrey. After a few minutes, they are all standing on the porch, waiting for further instructions.

"Hey, you kids come over here. We need more snow to finish the snowman. It looks like most of the snow is in the backyard. If we work on it together, we can get the snow moved to the front yard. It's probably going to take several trips, so are you guys up for it?"

The kids jump up and down with excitement and start maneuvering the wheel-barrel.

"Hon, Deb, and I will go inside to make hot chocolate and will catch up with you guys soon."

Aubrey asks if we can have a fire later so we can roast marshmallows.

"I think that is a perfect idea, Aubrey -- we will plan on it. Aunt Deb said she would get all of the ingredients ready for making s' mores, not just roasted marshmallows!"

It took a long time for them to bring the snow around to the front yard. We met up with them when we took a tray of hot cocoa outside. Nicole grabbed the Reddi-Whip whipped cream and started piping it onto the tops of the cups.

We feel normal again. At Deb's suggestion, we string white led lights up all over the new and improved snowman. He is six feet tall, has a perfectly round fat body, and looks mighty dapper. The lights outline his shape, and it's getting a little dark now, so they show up well. The finishing touch is a scarf, Nicole adds. What a great day!

Several weeks have passed again, but it seems like only yesterday when we were making that snowman. Mom said we had catered something like 50 parties so far this month, and we still have another week to go. Usually, when Caleb comes home for breaks, he needs to make money, so he pitches in at the kitchen. I know he wants to spend time with his friends, so we have given him Saturday off.

Anyone that has been in the food industry knows about the shenanigans that go on in the kitchen. Our kitchen is no exception. Every time Caleb comes home from college, we get to hear gross or funny stories of their shenanigans.

When my brothers, Jake, and Caleb all get together, the conversation almost always turns to use food as a prop for sexual body parts. After working long hours, we do let go. We like to have fun! Either they draw pictures of a penis or hairy vagina on the chalkboard.

When we are making pork or beef tenderloin – they really can act up. We purchase the tenderloins wrapped in sealed plastic, and they are about 18 inches long. The guys put them between their legs and dance around. Or to shock Mom and Carlos, they open them quietly and drain the liquid off. At that right moment, they would dangle it near their crotch area and lay it out on the stainless prep table. It shocks poor Mom and Carlos every damned time! I sense that we are not alone in this sick stuff. Other people talk about their kitchen antics, too. In our family, we have always been competitive and play around a lot.

We were lucky to have a swimming pool in our back yard from about the time I was in the sixth grade on, and it spoiled us. When we were teens and trying to grow up, Mom, of course, was always cooking, and Dad was at her side in a visible sous chef role.

She was in charge, but Dad didn't mind. His calm and joyous disposition kept her grounded. Dad made a huge grill, purposely located close to the pool area where they could keep an eye on us. God forbid, another child almost drowns in this family!

Our competitive streak came alive in the water. We would dive for hours and see who could get to the bottom of the pool the quickest, and how many water toys we could collect. Our swimming pool was deep, too. It had to be because we had a diving board. Our home had the only diving board I had ever seen in a backyard pool.

My favorite all-time water game was Chicken. You know the game—usually, the bigger of the pair holds the lighter person on their shoulders. Often with wobbly legs, you emerge with a fierce desire to win. It meant drowning your opponent.

My opponents were usually my mean brothers. They were

mean in the water because they wanted to win! However, I was older and wanted to win, and occasionally, they let me. Back and forth, sore necks, sometimes sunburned, it never mattered; the plans to play again and have a win was all that we could talk about at dinner.

I am super happy Caleb is here helping us with all the parties, but I know the time will pass far too quickly before he goes back to school. The planning for this year's holiday extravaganza started about two months ago! Along with other holiday type desserts, we plan to serve a variety of chocolate-dipped cheesecake lollipops. Caleb and Sue have been working hard all morning at rolling the cheesecake and flash freezing with lollipop sticks.

Once they set up, we will dip them with chocolate. Then comes the fun stuff: gold dusting and rolling them in smashed up peppermint or nuts and coconut.

Carlos yelled out for me to take a call. He said Meaghan was on the phone.

"Hi honey," I say, but all I hear is sobbing on the other end. "Honey, what is wrong?"

"Tia, it's my mom."

I look at Caleb, and he knows something is dreadfully wrong by the look on my face. "Meaghan, where are you right now, and where is your mom?"

"She is lying on the floor, and there is a lot of blood, Tia."

"Honey, I need you to hang up with me and dial 911. Caleb and I are on our way, and we will be there in less than five minutes. Meaghan, I love you, and your mom is going to be okay."

Without even speaking, Caleb heads to the sink to rinse his hands so he can go with me.

I holler out to Sue as I am leaving, "Go and tell my mom we had to go to Debbie's house, and she needs to wrap everything up and get to the hospital."

Caleb tells me that he will drive because I am upset. I do not have the energy to argue. Not even about the fact that he ran two lights getting to her house.

Caleb laughs a little and says, "Mom, can you believe we beat the ambulance?"

We run into the house just in time to see Deb walking into the kitchen.

She is wearing a faded robe, and I almost miss the blood trail because of the smell coming out of the kitchen. She had just finished making chocolate chip cookies when she felt blood running down her legs. Since Meaghan was in her room at the time, Deb thought she could quietly get into the bathroom to clean herself up before the timer went off for the cookies.

However, she slipped on the blood and fell on the tile floor. The tiles in her house have always been slippery, and I am pretty sure each of us has slipped on them at some point. Meaghan heard her fall, which is when she called me.

"Deb, what is happening, is it like before when you were in the bath?"

"No, it is worse," she replies.

We can hear the sirens, and Caleb runs out to meet them.

"Deb, we have to get you to the hospital, okay. You understand that, right?"

Without warning, she begins to cry. Not quietly this time. Her day was planned out; today, she wanted to be a normal mom and make cookies, make dinner, and then watch movies with Meaghan. All very normal stuff. She is standing in her kitchen, holding two trays of beautiful cookies. I begin telling her how great they smell when out of nowhere, she throws them across the room.

About that time, as Caleb leads the paramedics into the house, he glances over across the room to see the cookies broken and scattered all over. He commented that he was looking forward to eating one.

"Mom, I am picking them up and taking them with us."

On any other day, I would have thought that was funny. But not today. My humor is gone. We are attempting to get Deb loaded into the ambulance when I am ordered to retrieve all her medicine and follow them to the hospital.

Caleb takes control of the situation and tells Meaghan she can sit in the front seat, which means I get the backseat. It's not like I care, but I wonder where he got off ordering me around to the backseat of my own damn car. This feels like déjà vu! When I took her to the hospital a while back.

Why did I choose to drive her instead of calling 911? Today is not at all like before when we sat in the E.R. for hours waiting to be called back. My memories from that day are flooding in. It's the same, but it's not the same. Will the outcome be better or the same? My sister is fighting for her life! A short time after arriving, a nurse comes in and explains to us the rules on visiting. By now, we know the rules; another waste of time.

"Only two visitors at a time in one room; there is another person here to see our patient, so one of you must leave so she can come in."

"Caleb, can you go get Mimi please and tell her how to find us?"

A few minutes later, Mom arrives. When she walks in, you can tell she has been crying. She asks us what happened. Deb begins to explain to Mom, but suddenly, the doctors instruct us to leave the room. We quickly gather our purses and assure Deb we will be down the hall. I explain to Mom what happened and what I saw at Deb's house.

As we hold back the tears, I get that lump in my throat again. With sadness and worry, Mom announces that she needs to call the kitchen to get the staff organized for tonight's event and that she does not plan on leaving the hospital until Deb is out of the woods. Mom is relieved when I tell her I will take Caleb back to the kitchen and get the details lined out for the party before returning.

As we begin our walk down the long corridor to the elevator, Caleb slides his steady bony hand into mine. Somehow, at that very moment, my son became a man.

CHAPTER 17 – THE FAIRY IS YOU

Only a couple of hours later and Mom calls with an update. "Deb will be here for a while. She is bleeding internally, but right now, she is too weak for exploratory surgery. The chemo has done a number on her, and the doctors believe she has another infection in her blood. It may be due to the transfusions.

They are not sure about anything other than the fact that Deb is very sick." Mom also explains that they do not know what floor to put her on as she is not having surgery but needs constant observation.

"So, what does that all mean? Where will she be?"

Mom says, "It will probably be in the ICU again." She assures me she will keep me posted.

I promise to stay and work to make sure everything is good, but I will visit the hospital later tonight. Meaghan wants to stay with me for the rest of today, so I put her to work. The kitchen is busy, which will keep our minds off Deb for now. Mom is at the hospital, and I am worried about her, but she is strong, so I know she will be okay.

Ana was in the kitchen when Caleb and I got back; she is a source of comfort to Meaghan as Ana is the strong one right now. She watches over Meaghan like a mother hen and knows what to say and how to calm her down. Several hours have passed, and I begin to contemplate my next move.

We have significant events here at work all week, but I also need to be there for Deb. I want to be there more than here, but this is our livelihood, as well as the livelihood for so many employees. If we fail, they fail.

"Meaghan and Ana, let's wrap it up and get ready to leave. I want to go up to the hospital and see how your mom is feeling."

Ana follows me to the hospital. On the drive across town, the car is on autopilot. It knows the path too well. Our happiness earlier in the day before this hell started seems like a long time ago. I am beginning to feel the fatigue of it all and can assume it has just started again. It is different this time. Deb looks different. Should I mention to Mom that I think she looks different? Mom is sharply observant, so she's probably already thinking the same thing!

The space we live in does not separate us from one another as we are. In other words, I do not think of Deb as a daughter to our mom. I think of her as Deb, our family member that is loved equally by each of us. But that is not the case! We, each of us, have a different relationship and position with Deb.

She is my sister, so I guess that is the position I have. As we approach the parking garage, I am reminded again about my dread of being here. I hate this hospital because I have too many bad memories associated with it. Tonight, I will not be afraid to walk to the elevator, as I am not alone. Ana and Meaghan are with me. We are together in this.

As we approach the elevator, Michael, one of Deb's previous nurses, is standing there. He is sweet and caring. After hugging each of us, he asks if we are here to visit Deb.

"Yes, how did you know?" I ask.

"Because I am the lucky one -- the lucky one that gets to take care of my sweetie tonight."

The three of us try to hold back the tears. We want to be strong for Deb. However, when the lump in my throat becomes too large, I am unable to hold it in any longer. I blurt out some strange noise like a rumbled-up burp/fart combo.

Ana looks at me with her big brown eyes and tries not to laugh, but she can't help herself. Her reaction made us all laugh. A minute later, in the room, Deb tells us the doctors are concerned about the drop in her blood count and blood pressure. They are experimenting with how to get her blood count up because they have confirmed she does have an infection. Sepsis was a word used by the doctors when she was in here last time, but they eventually ruled it out.

This time they believe Sepsis *is* the cause of her bleeding, high fever, and low blood pressure. Sepsis can be a life-threatening complication caused by the body's responses to fight infection. Additionally, it can trigger a cascade of damage to the vital organs, which means they will eventually shut down and fail.

"So, how do we fight it?" I ask.

Deb says, "They started with strong IV antibiotics, and they are going to clean my blood with that big machine, like the last time."

"You mean, the 'Black Panther'?"

"Yes, see Denine, you do still have your sense of humor."

"Ha," I respond.

It's a form of dialysis. Dialysis is a familiar name to most people. It is usually a treatment for patients with kidney failure. Sounds like a good plan, but I know it can be dangerous, complicated, and will require a coordinated effort from a bunch of health care professionals. Is this staff up to it?

I know Michael, her nurse is, but what is his real skill set? I remember from last time that the machine has alarms that go off when something is wrong. And they went off quite a few times.

Deb is not healthy, and I worry if she will be able to pull through this time. I will not utter one word about my thoughts to another soul, and I will continue praying like crazy. Maybe I am cynical, or perhaps I have just experienced too much pain, and I only expect the worse. After all, when Bailey was screaming for joy from the snow, I panicked. Just for a moment, I assumed it meant something awful. I am sure I have PTSD.

To contemplate our future without my sister means we no longer can go through our day-to-day lives as we have previously done. Everything will be very different. In a big sad way! The depth of heartbreak will be tremendous.

My mom will be traumatized and never be the same

again; that is if she survives it at all. And the lives of Deb's two precious daughters will be destroyed. Deb dying is not an option; she *will* pull through this. Who dies from breast cancer at 39? No one in our family has. They were all in their 60s and 70s. I think Grandma was 65 when she died from breast cancer.

Here we go again with the idiots bringing in a food tray. Are you kidding me? I ask. If we all know she cannot eat anything, why don't they?

"I am going to go downstairs to get an iced tea. Does anyone else want anything?" I ask.

Ana hugs and kisses Deb and Mom and asks if I will walk her to her car on my way to the cafeteria.

The thoughts in my mind are crystal clear. Anything but that walk to the parking garage. I hate it. However, I say, "Sure, honey, let's go."

After Ana pulls her car out and heads down the hill to the bottom of the parking structure, I make a run for it. As I have done so many times before, I run down the stairs to avoid the scary elevator. Once I am back in Deb's room, my cell phone vibrates. It is Jake calling. He brought Bailey to the hospital to see Deb, and they are downstairs.

"Honey, don't you think you should have called me before you left the house? Deb is pretty sick, and I don't think Bailey should see her."

"Well, you are not in charge of everything, Denine. Bailey was crying for her, and I decided to bring her up here."

"Okay, I understand. I will run down to meet you in the lobby."

I explain to Deb, Mom, and Meaghan that Jake brought Bailey because she had been missing Deb.

Deb perks up and tells Meaghan, "Honey, get my scarf -- the one Bailey gave me."

It's purple and blue with bright red flowers. It's ugly, but Bailey chose it, so Deb loves it. Before I leave Deb's room, I tell her that I guess I will not be able to spend the night because Jake is dropping Bailey off now. Deb is okay with it and tells me that Meaghan is staying tonight so they can have their movie night together—the one they missed when this shit started. The hospital provides cable T.V. in each room, which I find strange – only because I am frugal. Tonight, I am thankful for it as they need this time together. *Mother and daughter.*

It feels later than it is. It is only 7:00 p.m., but it feels like midnight. When Bailey arrives, she asks Aunt Deb if she is smoking.

Deb tells her, "No, honey, I haven't had a cigarette yet, but I sure would like one."

Bailey tells her, "Then let's go and smoke."

My kid is smart. We die laughing because Bailey is snuggled next to Deb and looks like a baby due to her size. She is small for her age, and it is odd to hear her say, "Then let's go and smoke." While I ask Michael if we can take Deb down to smoke, I instruct Meaghan to get the wheelchair ready. Michael does not object at all. I expected some resistance, but he could not have been more agreeable.

He says to me, "This is not the time for her to stop smoking; she is dealing with too much and is pretty sick."

I laugh a little and reply, "Yeah, she's sick, so let's go smoke a cigarette."

He chuckles.

Mom explains that she will NOT be going down to smoke with us.

The hospital feels quiet tonight. We have not seen very much activity, so we probably will not have to deal with any rude people. We have been sitting outside for about two minutes when Bailey tells Aunt Deb how much she loves her and that she brought her a surprise. Deb smiles the biggest smile, then hugs Bailey and tells her she is her all-time favorite little person.

I am puzzled about the present as I didn't see anything in her hand when she got here. Bailey pulls out a tiny little fairy dressed in a beautiful white dress with gold trim. The top part has sparkles, and her hair is blonde. She begins speaking, telling

Aunt Deb that it is her.

"The fairy is you, Aunt Deb."

The lump is growing in my throat as Meaghan gets up to walk away. However, I saw her face before she turned her body. Her eyes were tearing up, and before I had time to take it in, she breaks down and is crying. You know the tears; they are salty and thick. Real tears that blind you and hurt your throat.

Bailey continues "Aunt Deb, her name is Deb, too, and she has magic powers that will help make you strong so you can leave the hospital. She is like your twin sister."

Meaghan is back, and we are huddled near Deb and crying.

Bailey is wondering why we are crying. She is happy and doesn't understand our sadness.

I explain that we are not sad. "These are happy tears, honey." Somehow, she believes me. It will take years for her to feel and understand the depth of this pain. Her legacy in the making.

Once done smoking, we head back into the hospital but only make it as far as the elevator doors when Deb starts projectile vomiting. For some odd reason, there is not a soul around —not even a desk clerk in the lobby.

Meaghan goes to hit the button on the elevator, but it is not working.

When we left Deb's room, we wrapped a blanket around her. She is now vomiting blood, and I use the blanket to try to hide as much of the blood as possible from the girls. I scream at Meaghan to keep hitting the buttons, but nothing happens.

Bailey is hysterical as Deb starts to stand up out of the wheelchair. Once standing, she begins a severe spell of violent vomiting. She has not eaten anything, and her stomach is full of blood. I knew we were in serious trouble and needed help.

"Bailey, I need you to stop crying and to sit down right here on the floor by Aunt Debbie. Bailey, do you hear me?" I demand.

She does not reply, but she does sit down and lowers her face into her hands. A sign of complete despair.

"Meaghan, I am going to run up and get Michael, so I need you to stay here with your mom and Bailey. Do not move!"

We are all freaked out, but thankfully, Deb sits back down; for a moment, she is not vomiting, so I make a run for the stairs. Due to the fucking elevator, I am mumbling under my breath every cuss word I can think of as I run up the stairs.

My legs are getting the best of me. Heavy. When I notice a number five on the wall. It may be the fifth floor, but that means ten flights of stairs. So, I have four more flights to go until I reach the seventh floor. As I fling open the door to the hallway, I am panting hard. My legs feel like bricks. I manage to run down the hall just in time to see Mom. She is sitting in the lobby waiting on us to get back to the room.

"Where is everyone? Where is Deb? What is wrong, Denine?"

"Mom, we need help, where is Michael?"

Mom says she doesn't know and starts running toward the nurse's station. She runs smack dab into Michael. By now, I am right behind her, and I smash my nose into the back of her head.

I blurt out, "Michael, Deb is vomiting blood, and the elevators are broke."

Michael and I hit the stairs again; we fly down to the lobby. When we get there, Deb looks alabaster pale and is sweating profusely.

She tells me, "Denine, you must be out of shape because you look like shit."

And then she laughs it off! We are sickos. My entire family is sick. We always laugh at the most inopportune times. As usual, Deb and I snicker, but Meaghan and Bailey are not laughing. *There is always someone not on board.*

Michael has access to a different "nurse/doctor-only elevator," which we pile into. After only a minute or so, we are back on the seventh floor. Mom meets us in the hallway.

Deb is acting weird and considering what just happened, kind of casual. To me, it's as if she is in a twilight sleep. We are ordered out of her room and gather in the lobby. I cannot stay here tonight as I have Bailey, and we have a crazy day tomorrow at work.

After chatting for a while, I agree to leave. Michael assures me she will be okay tonight, and it will take time to get answers to what is going on. Mom and Meaghan will stay at the hospital all night, and they have promised to call me if anything changes for the worse.

In the morning and after talking with Mom, we decide that I will go to the kitchen so she can be there with Deb. The plans are for me to work during the day and stay at the hospital at night so Mom can sleep. We will do our best to alternate until Deb gets a little more stable. The day goes by as expected, we got a lot of work done, and the employees have been fantastic. That is, everyone except for our new dishwasher. He chooses today to call in sick. Instead of waiting to hear what his reason is, I fire him. I tell him we need people who want to work. It was not until later that I found out his father had a heart attack and died before help arrived. He was the one that found him. I guess I get the award for the biggest bitch and have tried several times to reach him, but there has been no answer.

Carlos said he would go by his apartment after work today and offer an apology from me and to let him know he still has a job if he wants it.

After the last party goes out the door, I am finally able to sit and make a couple of phone calls. I first call Mom for an update on Deb. She says that Deb has had a pretty good day and that she spoke with the doctors. They are optimistic Deb will turn this around as her blood pressure is already better, and her fever almost gone. I also call to touch base with Jake.

He lovingly assures me that he understands what is going on and that he does not expect me home tonight.

"Honey, I will be home soon to shower and pack a night bag, so maybe we can sit and veg for a few minutes alone."

He tells me how much he loves me and that he will see me soon.

C HAPTER 18 – THE GUEST ROOM

A few more days have passed since Deb was admitted to the hospital for the fifth time this year. Her spirits seem uplifted. We have been laughing like schoolgirls all morning. She and I are sitting in her hospital bed, making way too much noise when a cranky old nurse comes in to scold us. To be clear; it was to scold me.

"How dare you behave this way in a hospital, in your sister's hospital room!"

Are you kidding me, lady?

Ms. Crotchety and I have crossed paths on numerous occasions, and neither of us like the other. She, however, as the nurse, needs to be kind to people. If she is too damned miserable with her own life, then why in the world would she continue working in this field? All of Deb's other nurses and doctors are amazing people. Amazing!

I slip off the bed and settle into the comfy chair that is right next to my sister. We continue laughing and reminiscing about our lives until they come in to take Deb for her MRI. I tell Deb I will be right here waiting for her when she returns. Tonight, is my night to stay with her. Deb's girls are planning on coming up later, too, so I hope we can keep the mood light, and our positive energy will continue to help Deb get strong. I feel confident that this time will be different. It just has to!

Jake has been working on our guest room at home so that when Deb is discharged from the hospital, she and Meaghan can come to stay with us, at least until she is healthy again. My love and respect for my husband is strong.

I know I have let him down as his wife, and it is abundantly clear to me that he is indeed my better half! It is hard to focus, and I find that I daydream more frequently. I pray for the day when we can lead boring lives. When my friends complain about their lives being too dull, I am flabbergasted and explain we should switch places. I cannot imagine loneliness or boredom, as my life has never been like that, even without cancer!

The vibration from my cell phone brings me back to reality. It is Cindy calling. She is trying to help and has offered to take Bailey for an overnight visit. Bailey loves her Aunt Cindy and Uncle Jason very much.

Later, when I saw Mom at the hospital, I told her, "Mom, I am staying at the hospital tonight with Deb, and the girls are coming up, too, for a little while. I am hoping you will stay home tonight and rest. You look like crap."

"Well, thank you, Denine. I can always count on you to make me feel good about my appearance," she says.

"Mom, I am sorry. It didn't come out correctly. What I meant to say is I am worried about you. You have been at the hospital every day and night, so I want you to rest if you can."

"I am grateful you will stay with Deb tonight, so I will stay in and rest . . . I promise."

Finally, it's my time to be alone with my sister. Everyone has left for the night. Just before the girls went, Deb got up and sat in a chair, which made all of us feel more relaxed about her condition.

To see her out of that bed meant the world to us tonight, and the only thing that would have made it better would have been to have Mom here, too, to see it. For the next several hours, Deb and I are alone, and it is quiet, other than the frequent interruptions to take her vitals and dispense drugs.

We are happy. Deb begins to tell me that she is worried about not having a Will. That puzzles me at first, but I soon realized that I would feel the same way if I were in her shoes. I could barely calm down the last time I had the lumpectomy because I thought I did not have my affairs in order. The last thing I remembered as they put me under was, "I pray I wake up."

"Do you think you need a Will now?" I ask.

"Honestly, I think it would have been a good idea when I was still with Russell, but I never got around to it."

"You don't have to worry about it, Sis, at least not right now. After you get home, we will get it done. You will not have to worry about it again after this."

"Denine, I want to tell you what I want to be done with my jewelry in case something happens."

It is very apparent to me that she is determined to have this discussion with me tonight, so I settle in and start taking mental notes. At one point, we are laughing about it, and I ask Michael if he is a notary.

"No, why?"

"Deb wants me to make sure her jewelry goes to the right people if she dies."

Michael tells her, "Nothing is going to happen to you anytime soon, Deb."

The last time I looked at my watch, it was 1:21 am. Deb has been napping for only a few minutes and is starting to toss and turn. A few more minutes pass when she sits up and asks for a cup of coffee. I walk down the hall to find Michael.

He says it will be okay if she has one and leads me to the nurse's station where they have a makeshift coffee bar. He also encourages me to have one too, points me to the "good" creamers in the fridge below, and hands me two real cups.

Once back in her room, I find her sitting in the chair again, which makes my heart jump with joy. This evening is going well. Deb is going to beat cancer this time, and she will get her life back! She has not been allowed food since she was admitted and has only been able to have clear liquids. This cup of coffee is just what the doctor ordered. Although a little restless, it is evident to me there are things she wants to get off her chest.

We are discussing the girls when out of nowhere, she tells me that the hardest part about being sick is wondering what will happen to her children and what it would do to Mom and me if she died.

"What will happen to my girls if I am no longer here?"

"Deb, why are you talking like this when it is obvious to me that you are going to be okay? Deb, you do seem better. I am not bullshitting you."

She explains to me that it is her wish, her dream to see her daughters grow up fully into adults and to see their dreams come true.

The thought of her dying terrifies me. She continues talking to me as if I were a colleague or neighbor. Not her sister. Now she is calm and more matter of fact. She tells me that if something happens to her, I need to be there to help Mom.

"I have always been there for Mom, and you, Debbie, and I do not plan on changing that, not ever. You can stop worrying about dying because, as Michael said, you are going to beat this and live a long life."

Her eyes tell a different story. I know she thinks she will not beat this. The battle has been hard. It's a sign only a sister can see. Through all our years together as sisters — in love and loathing at the same time — how am I expected to be able to go through the rest of my life without her?

Deb has been dozing on and off all night, and as morning approaches, she is sound asleep. Mom comes in quietly carrying goodies. Michael had called Mom to inform her that Deb is clear to eat again if she is hungry.

"Over the top" should be my mom's middle name. She has blueberry scones, apple butter and fresh fruit. She also brought a decanter of Pinon coffee with all the stuff that goes with it.

"Thank you, Mom; this is perfect for us, and is that Bailey's Irish cream?"

"Yes, I thought you might enjoy it."

"Mom, it is only eight o'clock in the morning; why would you think I need a drink?" I ask.

She ignores me. "How did last night go, girls?"

Deb tells Mom that it was a good night and that she had her first cup of coffee in almost a week. As I prepare to leave, I notice the look on Debs' face again.

She is calm and is no longer fearful. She seems at peace, which makes me wonder if we have passed another milestone in her recovery. Thank you, God, for answering my prayers - I am so very grateful in that moment!

Mom and Deb settle into a conversation, so I prepare to leave. Just as I get to the door, I turn around and tell them I love them both very much. They smile and tell me they love me, too, and I start to cry again as I walk alone down the hallway to the elevator. I also am at peace for the first time in as many days, so why am I crying again? I feel like our lives will get back to normal soon, and I am excited about my day today.

A few minutes later, I am on my way home to shower and get ready for work. We have six parties to deal with and are working for the most beautiful clients ever —no assholes in the mix. Each party has been on the books for months, and we know these folks very well. We have been catering for all of them for at least ten years.

We consider them our friends. Mom ordered stunning jewel-colored flowers for the trays. A couple of weeks ago we sugared pears, lemons, limes, oranges, pomegranates, and holly. The leftover sugared fruit still looks good, so we will get to reuse that, too.

As soon as I got home, I leaned over to kiss Jake and whispered, "Have I told you what a wonderful husband you are lately?"

"No, but you can tell me now because I have a surprise for you."

Jake grabs my hand as he leads me across the house to our guest room. The room is finished! He painted the walls a soft grey, and the five-inch baseboards a stark white. In the middle of the room are two antique twin beds dressed in pale yellow, pale grey, and charcoal colored bedding that has extra pillows, of course. Between the beds is a table that I have never seen.

It is wood and enamel and looks like an old telephone table with drop-down sides. It is whitewashed; very shabby chic, and a small glass pendant chandelier hangs above it. The old Kiva fireplace has also had a makeover. He tiled the lower part with what appears to be an ancient world, almost art deco style tile.

I am still not sure about it, but it doesn't matter, as it is gorgeous. The room is amazing! It is calm, sunny, and cheerful. I have been too busy even to notice the work happening in the room, which has caught me off guard. Had you asked me earlier when the room would be finished, I probably would have said it was weeks away. He has busted his ass in this room. He loves us, and I love him. It's a place fit for a cancer survivor; my sister will get healthy in this room, and Meaghan will get her mom back.

With that, I lead him into our bedroom. Bailey is at her dad's, so we have the house to ourselves, and I do not want to miss this opportunity to show my husband how much he means to me. On my way to work, I feel good about today. The chaos of December is almost over, and we can start to concentrate on Deb's recovery and get our family back on track.

As I pull up to the kitchen, I notice it is starting to snow a little. In the catering world, this means it is going to be a tricky day. But today is a good day, and we will figure it all out. I also notice that Karen is in the kitchen. She is a volunteer. She is lovely and brings a wealth of style with her. She is recently divorced and suffering on a grand scale. The ending of her marriage caught her off guard. She thought they were happy. She is my mom's age, but I treat her as if she is one of my girlfriends. She is both cool and uptight. I get a big hug from her just as I walk into the kitchen.

"Karen, you always make my day."

"Thank you, honey," she says. "How is Debbie?" she asks. She never calls her Deb.

"Deb had a great night, and it looks like she and Mom should have a pretty good day and possibly be able to go home soon. She wanted me to tell everyone hi. So, 'Hi' from Deb."

Two parties out the door and the pressure is on. The next four parties are the hard ones with extensive menus. Not complicated, just a lot of food. The phone rings, and as I reach for it, I spill an entire bowl of just-made cocktail sauce. Shit!

Mom hears the commotion and asks me what happened. As I am explaining to her, I get another call, so I tell her to hang on. In the meantime, I finish that call and forget she is holding on the other line, so she calls back.

She speaks with Karen for several minutes. Karen hangs up and tells me Mom wants me back at the hospital. She explains that Deb has started to run a fever, so they are watching her closely. I avoid going to the hospital because we have a ton of work to do today, and I am not willing to leave it to Sue and Karen.

Although I know they are both more than capable of making sure it gets done correctly. It is my responsibility, and I will see it through.

Besides, Mom tends to think the worst even more than I do, so she is probably just jumping the gun. Deb was more than fine when I left the hospital this morning! Mom calls again, and this time, I speak with her. She sounds worried but assures me everything is going to be okay. However, she does need me to get there as soon as I can. I explain that we only have two parties left, and I will get up there soon.

"Mom, Sue, and Karen will see the last two out, but I need to make sure the sauce for the lamb is perfect."

Jason typically makes the sauce, but he is stuck in the snow on the other side of the mountain. There is no hope he can get here to help because they just closed the roads in the canyon.

I explain to Karen and Sue what needs to be done with the two remaining parties when Mom calls again, ten minutes after the last call. There is panic in her voice this time as she explains the doctors came in and said Deb is not doing well, and her organs may be shutting down. At that, I hand over my files for the two remaining parties, and I run out the door.

I call Jake and Caleb on my way to the hospital. I explain to Caleb that he needs to find Meaghan and get her to the hospital. I tell Jake to get Bailey and get to the hospital as soon as possible.

I am almost to the hospital when I remembered that I did not call Ana, so I call her too. It goes straight to voicemail. I am reluctant to startle her, so I ask her to call me when she gets a break instead of leaving an alarming message.

As I pull into that parking garage, I feel an urgency to pee. I run to the elevator, and for the first time in a long time, I am not afraid to use it. I step in and start pushing buttons. The door stays open, and after a couple of seconds, I can tell it is not going to cooperate today.

"Of course, it's *not* going to work. Damn!"

Screw it. I make it to the stairs just in time as I need to clinch the pee. I hold onto the railing until the urge passes. Then I start walking fast. The restroom is just inside the hospital on the left side, so only a few more steps. I fling open the door, start unzipping my jeans, and barely sit down as it starts pouring out of me. Whew!

I missed a call from Mom while I was rushing to the bathroom. I am already in the hospital, so I don't waste time calling her back. When I step out of the elevator on the seventh floor, I noticed a large group of people standing near Deb's room. I cautiously walk down to where Mom is. Our eyes meet, and I see devastation. Mom is moving as if in slow motion and reaches out to hug me.

I push her away. "What the hell is wrong?" I demand.

No answer, so I walk past the huddled group and go directly into Deb's room and see her in the bed. Everything is fine. She is sleeping.

As I look up toward the ceiling, I blurt out, "Oh, thank God," all the while clenching my chest as if I could touch my heart. I am relieved to see her asleep. "Jesus Christ!" I scream out. "Mom, you scared the shit out of me! What the hell is going on here? Why is everyone acting so strange? And why are there so many people here?"

Michael walks around to me as he tells me she is gone. "Honey, Deb died a few minutes ago."

What?!? I can't breathe. It feels as if my life has just ended. The agony of our despair floods the room. How can she have died? I was just with her! Last night and again this morning - she was okay. She was better than she had been all week. How is it possible my sister is gone? There must be a mistake.

I glance over again at Mom. All I can think about is I need to go to her. I promised Deb I would take care of Mom. My mind wants me to move toward Mom, but my body is numb, and my legs won't move.

I finally make my way to the small couch and sit down next to Mom. We hug. I hold her tight while she sobs uncontrollably. For the first time in an entire year, I don't cry. I am frozen. I have nothing left in me.

We keep asking each other, "How did we not see this coming?"

Mom later told me that Deb died in her arms. She was sitting in the bed with her, holding her, and she quietly closed her eyes. It was peaceful for Deb . . . But not for our mother.

CHAPTER 19 – THE CARDBOARD BOX

Eventually, everyone that needed to be at the hospital arrives. One by one, they say their final, heart-wrenching good-byes. Some whisper secrets, should-haves, or utter regrets for not saying enough when Deb was still alive. Eventually, all of it stops. The hospital staff is professional. They're used to death. They give our family as much time as we need, and although Michael's shift ended earlier in the morning, he stays with Deb and our family.

As much as I am hurting, I cannot fathom the pain Mom and the girls were feeling. All I knew for sure is feeling the emptiness of my sister's absence is the only emotion we will never understand. How is it possible she is gone? We will never have another conversation. Everyone knows you are not supposed to outlive your children, and children are not supposed to be or-phans. It happens all the time, though.

My parent's immense grief shattered their hopes and dreams for their children and grandchildren to have a better life than they did. Each time Deb was at the hospital, one of us would walk with her as she was rolled to another area of the hospital. This hospital is enormous, so it took quite a while. We were not always allowed to go, but if we could, then we did.

The urge for me to walk beside her as they roll her out of the room this last time is too much to bear. The weight of our sadness is overwhelming. Where are they taking her? Will they handle her with respect? Do they know how much she is loved?

Our life once had so much promise. Even with all the trauma and drama from when we were little children, I thought we would survive my sister's diagnosis. I feel blindsided by all of this. Could we have asked better questions?

It feels disrespectful to pack up her room. She does not have much here -- an old sweater, a new, white robe with matching house slippers and stacks of get-well cards. And the ugly scarf Bailey gave her. It is hurting my heart to load it all up. Where will we take it? Where do we go from here? Bewildered, I sit down on the chair next to where my sister's bed once was. I am no longer able to hold my breath. I burst into uncontrollable sobs. None of us are prepared to handle this.

Mom has a huge house, and we immediately realize Meaghan cannot return to her own home. She will live with Mom for now.

It has only been a week since Deb passed, and we are going through the motions. The few remaining parties have been carried out by me, Jason, and our staff. Mom has been unable to step one foot into the kitchen.

Jason finally got through the canyon the next morning when the roads opened. He and I have been working side by side in total agreement and peace. The fight; punched out of us. I feel like I am desensitized by death. Or is it life? There is minimal conversation between us, only murmurs and stuttering. We don't have the energy. This muffled speaking causes us to keep asking each other, *"What did you say?"*

Our ability to function even at a basic level is difficult. Food no longer tastes good. Sleep never comes. The fact that we still have our circle of friends is shocking because we are disconnected.

Our only goal is to finish December and prepare for Deb's funeral. It has not always been natural or second nature to love my brothers, but as I stand in the kitchen next to Jason, torn by grief, chaos, and confusion, I realize he and I are more alike than I thought. I love him, dearly, and miss Matt. I need him here.

Our shared tragedy forces us to fight to remember every good memory we have of our sister. And it reminds us to *remember* our love for each other too. The time wasted in the kitchen by either too much estrogen or too much testosterone is behind us now. There will be no more food fights. That's the past.

We have lost everything. This is our new beginning. Our lives are complicated, but we are survivors -- a trait we learned from our mother.

As if we are newbies at event planning, we stumble through the plans for Deb's funeral. We make our living planning and executing very successful, high-society parties, but planning a funeral for our beloved daughter, sister, mother, and aunt — well, that is another story.

Deb shared her wishes with me the night we talked about her jewelry. We talked about a lot of stuff, including the fact that she wanted to be cremated. She did not belong to a church, but she was a spiritual person, so it seems like an obvious choice to have the memorial at Mom's house. That is about as far as we get in our plans.

We know we must have food and that someone needs to speak, but how that will happen is anyone's guess. When I think back now to the night before she died, it is clear to me that Deb knew she was dying, which is why she needed to be sure I knew her wishes regarding her jewelry and her other stuff. The girls split almost everything, as they should.

Mom would get the beautiful butterfly pin she had made for Deb the year Meaghan was born, and I am supposed to get her set of emeralds. Big fucking deal. I want my sister back. Over the years, money would come and go in Deb's checking account, but she never changed the way she lived. It made her more grounded.

My point is this: her jewelry meant a lot to her, and in her eyes, it would mean a lot to the girls when she passed. They would treasure it, and it would serve as a reminder of her love. She had nothing else to give. There would never be another conversation with either daughter, and she hoped that what she had already taught them would be enough to carry them through and to know the depth of her love for them. The jewelry was a distraction from our conversation about the girls. I know that now.

Deb's main concern was for them. How would they deal with her death? How would Meaghan handle no longer being able to live in the home she had known for so long? Now I realize why the hospital staff said she could eat and drink anything she wanted...why Michael didn't object to her smoking, eating, or drinking.

He knew she was dying. I hate Michael right now. The asshole should have *told* us she was dying. Armed with that knowledge, I would have said something more meaningful to her. It would have mattered to my sister.

Matt needs to hear about Deb from someone that loves him, and Dad is the best candidate for this. Mom and I were grateful that we did not have to make the drive to the prison or be the one to look into Matt's eyes when he heard that Debbie died.

"There are no visits allowed during the week; it is Monday, so who is here to see me?" he asked the guard.

When Matt saw Dad's face, he knew the news was grim. "Deb did not make it, son. She passed away."

Matt would not be allowed to leave for the funeral service; he grieved alone – in dark silence. Matt yearned to be home; his days were almost unbearable. Regret was eating him alive as he knew there would be no 'do-overs."

While in prison, Matt was changing for the good, but he still knew he would have to deal with the issue of his addiction once he got out. The day Dad walked into that prison to tell him his sister died; Matt knew he would never be tempted by drugs again.

He once told me that he felt like a total loser. "I wish I could have been there to help Deb and to help you and Mom. I would have made a difference for you guys. The drugs will never retake hold of me like they have my whole life."

Another reality check for Matt was that with Deb gone, he only had me. We were the last of the three "first" kids born. We knew each other intimately, better than any other living soul. We kids, the first three, were what I always called the bastard side. Mom knew her favorite was always Jason -- the youngest. When we were young, it worked in our favor. We had tons of time and freedom to run the neighborhood streets until dark.

"Matt, you are loved very much by us, and you were loved very much by Deb. She would light up when we talked about you or when you would call her. You have to believe and know in your heart that she loved you very much."

Another day passed before we were able to discuss the actual funeral. Mom is numb. She spends most of her time crying and lying down in her bed. I don't know what to do. Again, I go through the motions. Each day I leave the kitchen and return to Mom's, only to find myself lost. My pain cannot be worse than Moms. After all, Deb was her child. But I am dying inside. I feel like I will explode one day if the backed-up pain cannot escape my body. It's like a blood blister that needs to pop to release the pressure.

Several friends and family members have been at the house almost 'round the clock since Deb died. The one thing we can all agree on is our friends. We are blessed. Each of us has a group of amazing friends.

We also have *shared* friends. Lori is one of those people. Lori lovingly sends food every day. The two fridges are overflowing. Not that we can enjoy it, but it feeds the many visitors that flow in and out.

I remember when I first met Lori. I thought, "Wow, that is one beautiful lady." I feel like we are all friends with her now. Over the years, we have become close from catering for her and with her. She is married to a kind man. He has always corrected me, insisting I call him by his first name. He has one of the sweetest dispositions I have ever met. They have money, but their wealth is not what defines them. It is more about their generous spirit. Lori makes sure that we have everything we need, from food to desserts, for several days. It is the good stuff, too, as Lori is an accomplished chef in her own right.

Whenever I see or hear Lori's name, I am reminded of the funny story about our cake. She loves it, and she will do and has done, just about anything to get it. Years ago, Mom lived on the same street as Lori.

Before Mom left for New York to vacation, she called Lori to tell her she had left her a large piece of cake and that Jason would let her into the house to get it. Lori waited several hours for Jason to get home, and when she could no longer stand it, she called Mom to ask if any windows were unlocked so she could climb through to get her cake. Mom laughed and told Lori to try the window near the laundry room. "If it's open, feel free to climb in."

Lori told Mom, "And if it isn't, I am going to break the window so I can get that cake! I will, of course, get the window fixed."

We have laughed about that story for years. Lori did not have to break any window since Jason left the back door unlocked.

My ex-husband Chris was close to Deb. Much to my dismay, they stayed in contact, so it seems natural to let him help now. He is distraught and wants to be involved. Since Mom financially supported Deb after Russell left, it will also be Mom who pays for her funeral.

Chris has instructions about what to do at the funeral home, so I pray he doesn't screw it up. Armed with a blank check, he goes there to handle the final arrangements.

Etta is another great family friend. She wants to help in some way, so I ask her to help write the obituary. Putting complete sentences together is not happening for me right now. Etta writes a lovely paragraph, and I am relieved she can do this for us. A paragraph is not much, but again, what more can one say to explain how much we will miss her and how deep our love is for Deb?

While talking with Mom, Bailey ran into the room to tell us that Jason and her daddy were fighting.

"Honey, what are they fighting about?"

Bailey blurts out, "Mommy; Aunt Debbie is in a shoebox."

As Mom and I head down to the garage, we ran into Jason,

who was pissed. Jason explains to us what happened, and I found it funny. Disturbing, but funny.

With tears in his eyes, Jason snapped at me, "I fucking don't think it's one bit funny, Denine. You are always laughing at the wrong time. I have never understood how you and Deb can laugh at every goddamn thing ever said. What the fuck is wrong with you, anyway?"

He rarely if ever uses the F word, so I know he is distraught. At that very moment, I realize the reason we laugh. It's our coping mechanism. Laughing makes life more tolerable. Now we are all corralled like horses in the garage, trying to figure out this mess.

Chris did what Mom told him to do. He went to the funeral home to retrieve the ashes and settle the bill. Chris didn't know how or what to do differently, so he allowed the funeral home to direct him. He showed up with a plain cardboard box containing my sister's ashes.

Jason was pissed off and very upset that Chris did not think it through. "You had a blank check, dude," he says.

"It wasn't the money, Jason. I didn't know what to do. That is how they gave her to me."

"So, your best decision was to do nothing and bring Debbie home in a fucking cardboard box! Did you think that would be okay, Chris?"

It is funny, and Deb would have thought so, too, but I agree with Jason. Chris should have bought one of the urns at the funeral home. If we didn't like it, we could have made the switch, but at least her remains would not be in a cardboard box.

No one thought this through. In the movies, you see the loved one's ashes placed in a beautiful urn or vase resting on the fireplace mantel, but in real life, you do not consider how those ashes ever got into the container. In a fury, Jason pushed by us to get the keys to Deb's house from Mom's room. He knew she had a couple of gorgeous hand-carved vases at her home. He was taking charge.

After a couple of hours, Jason returned with a pink, gold,

and turquoise vase. As it turns out, it was one of her favorites and hand-painted by an old Indian neighbor of hers. She had always cherished it and her friendship with the man. He was 90 when he passed away last year. How did Jason know this vase was her favorite?

Next came the tough part. Jason had to transfer her ashes from the shoebox into the vase. I imagine the memory is forever etched in his mind. I later learn that he handled the ashes very carefully. He used a wooden spoon like the one he and Matt were spanked with when they were little boys.

Scoop after scoop; he carefully transferred the ashes until the jar was full. He sealed it with the lid and brought it upstairs where it stayed. It was placed on our mother's fireplace mantel. I assume the wooden spoon went straight into the dishwasher.

C HAPTER 20 – WOODEN SPOON

My friend Cabrini asked me the other day how Jason transferred Deb's ashes into the vase. I explained about my ex's failure at the funeral home and how he and Jason got into a huge argument. I start to tell her that he used a wooden spoon, but before I can complete the sentence, I can see she is a little mortified.

I elaborate, when my brothers were younger and acting up, Mom and Dad would grab a wooden spoon and swat them on their butt. For some reason, they would not get washed afterward. Instead, they returned them to the fat jar that sat next to the stove. It was full of wooden spoons and spatulas. So, using it to transfer Deb's ashes made perfect sense to me, and it must have to Jason as well.

Cabrini suffered the loss of her mom last year, which devastated her. She is empathetic to suffering and is probably the kindest human I know. She loves big time and has a great spirit. She married Fred at a young age, and they remain happily married today. I love Fred, too. He is an awesome man and a great husband. The four of us go camping as often as we can. We eat, drink too much, and ride four-wheelers. Now that I think about it, it has been over a year since our last trip. I trust Fred with my life and respect him. He stands firm in his convictions, which I appreciate.

I am close to all my girlfriends' husbands. Bill is married to my friend Carolyn, and another love of mine. They are madly in love and living their dream life together. She is always his priority, and she cannot imagine her life without him in it. We have all learned much from Bill. He is a very dignified man with a dry sense of humor.

Deb's memorial is tomorrow. We have pulled ourselves together, and I think the details have been worked out. I wonder how we will get through the day. How will Mom and the girls survive? I am sad just thinking about it all. We have decided to let Uncle Gary, who is my aunt Myra's husband, say a few words and then open it up for anyone else that has something to share. He is a minister, so he will probably say a prayer too. What could I say about my sister that would relay how wonderful she was?

Caleb and Jake are getting ice to fill the buckets for drinks, and I still need to go to the kitchen or store to get napkins, plates, and cups. Dianee is another great friend, and as she reminds me to grab a large coffee maker when I get to the kitchen. I realize just how blessed we are.

As I ponder the many friends who have shown up for us, I think back to when Dianee first came into our family. She knew everyone in town and was a good connection for us business-wise. But over the years, she has moved into the position of an extended family member. We see her at our baby showers, holiday parties, and just about any other occasion. It is natural to see her in our homes.

She tells me to stop worrying about it all. "Denine, what has been forgotten will not be remembered." She is a very wise woman and has a knack for calming us down. Suffice it to say, we all love her.

The kids put together a picture board last night after raiding our collective photo albums. They did a great job, and the collage of photos is our evidence Deb had a good life full of love. There was enough suffering along the way, too, which made the good days great days. Aunt Myra wanted to help with the food, so she made blue corn chicken enchiladas, and Aunty (what our family calls Myra's mom) made her salsa. Not just any salsa, mind you. Hers is the best! She should have sold the recipe years ago.

Aunty has always worked hard and had a hard life early on. When I was about 16, I grew close to her when we cleaned offices together. I am unsure why she did that. I never knew if it was for extra money, or to supplement an existing income. I have a memory of her pantry and cabinets being as full as they could be. She never ran out of anything! Not ever. She was thrifty and a fantastic cook, too. Fifty years ago, life was different. You grew your own food. The original farm-to-table movement started in the '40s and '50s. She learned to cook using the very best, freshest ingredients.

Flower and fruit bouquets have been arriving all morning, and now we have enough food to feed a small army. It's always about the numbers when you are in the catering business. Mom's house is about 3,000 square feet, and I hope every inch is filled with people. I am praying for a great turnout. To have a good turnout means Deb was loved. I can't imagine dying and having no one attend your funeral other than your immediate family. I am as close to my friends as I am to my family, and they mean just as much to me.

The service will start when everyone gets here. Etta put in the obituary that it is to start at 11, but it will begin when everyone arrives. We do not need to rush this; Mom remains in her room, lying in her bed, crying. In my rush to get the paper goods and finish our last party yesterday, I completely forgot about what I would be wearing.

Again, I've screwed up. Quick and dirty is my style. I do not own an appropriate black dress, so on my way back to Mom's from the kitchen, I will run into Target to see what I can find. Fortunately for me, I ran into Carla.

Carolyn, Carla, and Cabrini. My small circle of support. Carla was married to Bruce, who lost his battle to cancer. She, too, has been through the roller coaster of grief. I continue to learn so much from her. She has the same grace her husband had during his fight with cancer. I have always believed the adage, "Sisters by chance, friends by choice." This is true of my friendship with these three women.

Carla asks me why I am running through Target. I explain that I forgot about getting a dress for the memorial; she immediately knows what to do. "I will help you look, but if we do not find anything, my house is on the way to your mom's. Denine, I only own black dresses, and I know I have one that will work for you."

"Who forgets stuff like this?" I ask her. I feel so guilty. My sister meant everything to me, and this is how I honor her? Jake and Caleb have new suits, and Bailey has a new dress.

"My hair is a mess, and I have nothing to wear."

I am having a nervous breakdown in the middle of Target, and Carla is trying everything to calm me, but all I can think about is I have nothing to wear and am running out of time. Just like my ex-husband Chris, I've failed. This is who I am. Jake is right. I am too "quick and dirty."

I am standing there in the middle of Target using the bottom of my shirt to wipe mascara from my cheeks when I notice that we are standing close to the aisle where they have the greeting cards. I also see a package of birthday candles. I start laughing, hysterically. I pick up several packages of candles and kept laughing. I am now crying and laughing all at the same time. A few minutes pass when I am sure Carla thinks I have lost my mind.

I finally collect myself enough to explain why I am losing it. "This is who I am, Carla. I regularly forget important things. When Caleb turned 16, I had been running around like crazy, just as I have been today. I made a nice dinner and cake but forgot to buy candles."

After all, birthdays are all about making a wish and blowing out the candles, right? We were just about to sing happy birthday when I discovered I had no birthday candles! We only had scented candles in jars. I was in panic mode when I noticed the magnets on the fridge. There were numbers and letters. I pulled off the one and the six and pushed them down into the frosting on top of the cake. We sang happy birthday to Caleb, and he blew out the scented candles on the table. Caleb was not disappointed, but I was.

"I am buying all of these packages of candles, so I will never run out of them again," I quip to Carla.

Carla and I do not find a dress, so I borrow one of hers. It fit me perfectly, and as it turned out, *the dress didn't matter at all*.

Our family's sadness was overwhelming, but we managed to get through the day with a little dignity and a whole bunch of love. It was standing room only, and we went through almost all the food. The day turned out better than expected, and the girls made good connections with well-meaning friends.

Now, what do we do? Where do we go from here? Although I should have paid more attention to everything, I was lost and crippled with despair. As I write this down, I only vaguely remember what the weather was like on that day. And I know we had flowers and well wishes from many people, but that also escapes my mind. I can't remember if we ever sent out thank you cards.

I miss my sister. How will I survive this? *I am very grateful she is no longer suffering,* but I want her back here with us. I need one more chance to sleep by her side. To hold her hand and to tell her what she meant to me and how much it meant to have her as *my* sister. I know she knew how I felt about her, but I should have said it more often.

Now comes the enormous task of emptying Deb's house. Russell showed up for the service and "authorized" us to go any-time. I find that insulting. After all, it has been all of us who were there for Deb, not him. He couldn't take it. He ran away, and now he is interested in helping. Or is he just interested in the house and everything that is in it?

After discussing it in great length, we have decided to go to Deb's sooner rather than later, because they were still married, and she was never able to get anything done legally about her share of the assets.

We plan to go on Saturday, which is a couple of days away. Aunt Myra suggests that we make a list of what we want to take out of the house. Ana and Meaghan have a limited idea about what they would like to get, but no one else does, which means we are "winging it."

Most of the southwestern pottery and framed art is Mom's or was given to Deb by Mom, so we should plan on getting it out of there. I want one or two of her plants. The entire jewelry box will be taken to Mom's house. I have no idea when anyone can go through it, but it needs to be at Moms for safekeeping.

We also agreed that we should take Deb's ashes to California to the ocean because she had mentioned that a long time ago. In the spring, we will drive to California. We cannot go to California without visiting Disneyland, so we will make it sort of a vacation, too.

The only problem with it is Jake has exhausted his vacation/PTO days, so he is unable to go, and neither can Mom. Ana also only has a couple of days open, so she will have to fly out. Caleb, Meaghan, Bailey, and I will drive. In my entire life, I never thought I would say, "We will take Deb's ashes to the ocean and then go to Disneyland." Again - surreal.

Saturday came too quickly. Dad came to help us, also, which was a good idea. Russell will not cross Dad and will keep his distance from me. I detest him and want nothing to do with him. He made Deb's life harder than it already was, and I have cursed him daily. Due to his weakness, he was unable to support her and the girls. He bailed on them, and now he wants to be part of this.

He wants to know what happened in the end and is asking us all sorts of questions.

"Russell, do you think it is okay for you to ask me what happened? She died, that's what happened. She died, and you were not there. You turned her life into a nightmare, and she did not deserve any of it!"

It didn't take long before he realized that he was *unwelcome* in his own house. He had been gone too long; almost the entire year that my sister was sick, he was checked out. Now, at best, we are casual acquaintances; and no longer family. Not to him.

The day he walked out on my sister was the last day we were his family. His daughter does not respect him and resents what he did to her mom, who was the only true mom she ever had. Deb loved her very much. There was never a question about how close they were. It was as if Ana was always her daughter.

After four or five hours, we finished walking the halls of the empty cold house. Closets were emptied, and furniture and decorator items were all loaded into the moving van.

Dad is always dignified and respectful, and this day was no different. To my dismay, he shook Russell's hand before we walked out onto the porch to leave. Russell assures him that if he finds anything that we missed, he will call us.

Liar! He plans to sell the house. It is scheduled to go on the market within two weeks. Additionally, he announced, **by accident**, that he is getting married. What a pig. Good luck with that, lady – whoever you are!

Dad's respect turned to a curt goodbye, and we all pulled away from the little house in the valley that was my sister's home for so many years. I was quite sure that I would never return or even drive down her street again.

The phone rings. It is from Matt. He will be released in two weeks, and I am ecstatic. Mom spends most of her days crying, and today is no different. I am so happy for him but sad that he was unable to be here for Deb's memorial. He missed it by a few weeks.

Matt will live in a halfway house for the first six months so they can monitor his every move and see how he transitions back into his life. I know he will do well, and we are all eager to hug and love on him.

Now that Deb is gone, he will fill that void a little, and maybe when he gets released from the halfway house, he can stay with Mom or Dad. They could both use his help around the house. And, of course, there is always the guest room in our home.

Jake and I were chatting this morning about the trip to California. He thinks it might be useful if Matt goes with us since he missed the memorial. I would love that, but I am not sure Matt can get permission from his probation officer to leave the state.

In an earlier conversation, Matt explained to me he must jump through lots of hoops during the first six months. Random pee testing will become routine, as well as an early curfew. He must be back at the house by 8:00 p.m. every day. A significant requirement is to find a job within a week, which luckily for Matt is not an issue, because he will work with us.

Fortunately, the halfway house is only about two or three miles away, so it will be easy for us to pick him up and drop him off. In Mom's absence, Jason and I are relieved to have another capable set of hands. We are unsure when Mom will be able to return to work, and we will not put any pressure on her. To lose a child is unspeakable pain.

The pain I feel seems to be severe, even crippling at times. As Deb's sister, my pain must be different from Mom's. Grief is a messy emotion. One might say, even ugly.

I don't care about much these days. Some days my anger gets the best of me. I feel I should have done more. I find myself blaming the doctors for not saving her. I never thought this would happen, and I always knew in my heart that she would recover. But she didn't. We lost her, and there is nothing any of us could have done that would have saved her. Now we must protect ourselves and our children. Our unbelievable circle of friends never let us down. They do not just show up for the good times and the food. They actually "show" up in our lives when we need them the most.

After having a brief conversation with me, one of my mom's dear friends stopped by earlier today to encourage Mom to get out of the house. Mom has been friends with her for something like 35 years. While Mom and Dad still lived in Roswell, Mom would drive to Albuquerque to get her face done.

That is how they first met. Diane (not to be confused with

our other family friend – Dianee) does facials and aesthetic services. Several years ago, she started working with a local cosmetic surgeon. — I feel a bond with her, even though we never get the chance to spend much time together. Although she is fit and looks great to me, she wanted a breast lift. I am not sure if something went wrong, but she describes her new size as a 42 long. Anyway, she is a rock of a human, and our family adores her.

Diane found Mom sitting outside on her deck, still in her pajamas and wrapped in a warm blanket. She is numb from the pain, but not from the cold. Mom had been eating junk food and drinking wine, as evidenced by the wrappers thrown all over the place, and several empty wine bottles found tucked under the wobbly and weathered antique table. What I do know now is this is going to take a long time. The grief is eating her alive and has a firm hold on her heart.

When will Mom return to work? How will I manage to deal with all the pressures of trying desperately to fill her shoes? When will I be permitted to grieve? What will happen tomorrow? Where in the hell do, we go from here?

C HAPTER 21 – I WILL SEE YOU IN MY DREAMS

Over the past year, my friends have grown weary of my turmoil and sadness. One of them even had the nerve to ask, "When do you think you will get over it?"

"Get over what?" I asked.

She started to say, "Get over your sister's death," but before she could finish those words, I jumped down her throat and told her that if she could not comprehend that I will never get over it, then she should probably find a new friend. She was very apologetic and explained it was out of concern for my well-being that she brought it up in the first place. "My well-being is the least of my problems."

For some, there is a preconceived idea that grief is like any other ailment. It has a timetable: a beginning, middle, and end. That it might be like maternity leave following the nine months of being pregnant, once that time passes, you return to work and resume your old routine. The only logic about that is when you go on maternity leave, it is because you had a baby, which is a gift at the end of the nine months! Death isn't a gift. When you lose someone you love, six weeks is not enough time to heal your heart and to "get over it." It just doesn't work like that. Right? Is that how we should regard grief?

I assumed Deb would be part of my life and in my life for the rest of my life. Our lifelong secrets will now live on in me. Once upon a time, I assumed all my siblings, and I would grow old together. But that is not reality. When asked how I am doing, the conversation quickly turns to, "How are your parents?" Or, "How are her daughters doing?" At times, that makes me angry.

"How am I doing?" is the question I want to be asked and given a chance to talk about it. Therefore, I keep most sentences short. Maybe this is God's way of helping me figure it all out.

Every day is a small victory in putting my life back together — one foot in front of the other. I look forward to our road trip. I plan to ask the kids how they are doing and encourage them to open up as they can. They have permission to be happy, crazy, angry, and do whatever they need to so they can also continue putting one foot in front of the other.

Bailey is growing up with her best friend, Reed. They are very close, and I could not have gotten through so much drama over the past year without the help from Stacey, Reed's Mom. She knows just what to say and when to offer support. She has had Bailey quite a lot, and I never worry or think twice about it. I love Reed the same. She is my other daughter.

Jake asked Stacey to take Bailey again tonight, as her dad is out of town until tomorrow, and he has a surprise for me. I usually hate surprises, but not this one. He made a reservation at the resort.

He tells me, "The resort heals everything, right, hon? We will check into the resort early tomorrow, and then you and the kids will leave for California two days later."

How do I deserve *this* man? We have not even kissed since my sister died, which seems strange to me. At times, I wonder what Jake thinks about our life together now? Before Deb got sick, we were always kissing and holding hands.

My favorite time together was slow dancing in the living room after everyone else had gone to bed. I am fortunate, too, that we always talk. We will not be one of those couples you see in restaurants, eating in silence.

Intimacy with my husband has never been an issue until now. I feel weird, and it seems like a guilty pleasure. My sister did not have anyone to intimately love her during the last several months of her life. It doesn't seem right to me. I know it is, but I feel guilty for having someone like Jake in my life. While watching the sunset, we enjoyed a bottle of wine and realized I was finally feeling relaxed. Jake ordered something I have never tried. He has a good sense of what I like, and his choice was excellent. Later we made love and fell asleep in each other's arms. I am not alone, and I am lucky to have Jake in my life.

The California travel day is finally here. I asked everyone to pack light since we will only be gone four or five days. It's California, and after checking their weather for the week, I was happy about the unusually high temps all week.

Just as I am trying to leave, the phone rings. *Of course, it does*! As soon as I answer it, I realize it's not bad news, no dread this time. It is Mom telling me she loves me and wants us to call her every day with an update on how it's going.

She also needs to give me Ana's flight information. Jake gives us all one more kiss before we pull out of the garage. Matt was not able to get permission to go with us. It will be just the kids and me. He and Jason will hold down the fort at work since Mom has not been able to return yet. Caleb will help drive. I am saddened as I drive away from our home. Jake and I reconnected at the resort, and now I am going to be gone for almost a week. I already miss him.

Bailey interrupts my thoughts when she blurts out, "Mommy, Meaghan is crying."

I do not need to ask why. I know why she is crying. Her mom's ashes are traveling with us to California. Bailey sits next to her, and her tiny, little hand keeps patting the top of the vase.

Caleb rolls his eyes and tells me, "You are all a bunch of freaks. Mom had I known we were taking her ashes in our car; I might have decided not to come along. It's a little creepy," he says.

Some people might find it creepy, but I didn't, and neither did Bailey. It puzzled her at the very beginning, but now she seems comfortable with it. Bailey asks if she can move Aunt Deb so she can lie down. Before I have a chance, Caleb tells her no.

"Bailey, you have to stay in your seat belt. You cannot lie down."

I ask myself what I could have been thinking about when I

agreed to this trip. Maybe Caleb is right. It didn't seem strange at the time, and even Mom thought it was a good idea. I hope this is not another mistake — a horrible nightmare.

After driving for about five hours or so, we agree to pull over to stretch our legs while refueling. Bailey grabs Meaghan's hand and asks her to take her to the potty. When they leave, Caleb and I talk about how "it's" going.

"Meaghan is dealing with the reality of never seeing her mom again. I am concerned with what and how we will pour her ashes into the ocean."

Caleb says, "Mom, how will we do that? Have you ever done anything like that?"

"No, not ever! But I am sure we will figure it out."

Back on the road, and both girls are asleep, which is good for me. At least they will not be cranky when we get to L.A. It's been a pretty easy drive, more relaxed and more uneventful than I thought it would be.

About an hour after we left home, Caleb took over. He drove the first part of the trip because I did not want him driving into L.A., so now he is my navigator. I kind of know where we are going, as we have been here many times before, but everything looks a little different. I am not scared to drive here, but everyone is going at least 80 miles an hour, and that bugs me.

For as long as I can remember, my love for road trips has topped the list of my favorite thing to do. I look forward to them. In fact, after returning home every time from a trip, life is different. Not better, just different. Meaghan is finally smiling for the first time since leaving Albuquerque.

"Tia, this hotel is beautiful! Oh my gosh, look at the pool and the palm trees! Is that a swim-up bar in the water?"

"Yes, that's what it looks like," I answer.

I didn't know it was this nice when I made the reservation. I chose the place because it was close to the beach. I instruct the kids to hang out while I check us in. When I return, I tell them I have a surprise.

Bailey is so excited. "Mommy, what is it?"

"You have to wait and see, honey. Let's get up to our room."

We unloaded everything out of the car, including Deb. On the rolling cart, Meaghan had her wedged between suitcases and purses. Based on the look on his face, I assumed Caleb thought she should have stayed behind in the car. As soon as we enter the room, we hear the ocean. It was a warm night, but I had asked the staff to open the patio doors so that when we walked in, the kids would be surprised. They were stunned! Our ocean view room on the tenth floor was so far the best part of our journey. I was left alone as they all ran to the balcony.

It was larger than I thought, and the smell and the sound of the waves hitting the shoreline were magical. A lighthouse or some other structure lit up the water, and they figured out we were right on the beach. Would this be Deb's final resting place? It was important to me that this trip be a memorable one.

Not just because of Deb, but maybe for new beginnings for us all. We need some happy memories instead of doom and gloom. Meaghan needs a reason to survive. Her heart is broken. She wishes her mom was here with us in a different way, not in an urn. Although I know Meaghan knows her mom is no longer suffering, I am not sure she understands what happens to your body after you are cremated.

I had to find out myself after Chris brought Deb home in that damn paper box. First, the funeral home places the ashes, which include bone fragments into a heavy-duty plastic bag. The bag then is put into the cardboard box. Why in the hell did they not offer him an urn? Idiots. Cremation doesn't hurt. The person is dead. The body doesn't feel pain. The thought of a body burning is the horrific part to me, so I am sure there are unanswered questions in Meaghan, Caleb, and Bailey's mind.

Meaghan's grief is getting the best of her, and I know she has no control over her thoughts. I hope the fact we are going to discuss it will help. I pray I say the right thing and hope that we can have an open discussion about the process and the unanswered questions.

Instead of sugar coating it, I try to be as honest as I can with the kids, even though I did not want to scare them in the process. I ask if they wanted to see the ashes. "It is your choice, and I do not want to force you."

This moment is about them, *only* them. Thankfully, the conversation goes much better than expected, and the only one interested in seeing the ashes was Bailey. I let her touch them, and she even smells them. Later, I hear her tell Meaghan, "she" didn't stink. It makes me feel weird, and I must remember it is Bailey that said that, but more importantly, I want to see Meaghan's reaction to the comment. If Meaghan is upset, she doesn't show it.

In the morning, I am awakened by coffee in bed, just like home. Close to tears, I thank each of them with a kiss and a hug. Caleb plays it off, but I know he is feeling something. He is different now, too.

I need to stay strong, but moments like this take my breath away as I have the best kids anyone could have, and Meaghan is like a daughter to me. She is an old soul. I feel like I knew her in a former life and cannot imagine being closer to any other group of kids in this life. I am working on getting closer to my stepchildren, but their mother makes it virtually impossible with her constant antics. They are my future, and I hope to be able to focus more on them when we return home.

"So, guys, what do you want to do today?" I ask.

In Caleb's silence, I can tell he wants us to do what Meaghan wants to do. I am agreeable with anything and waffle between happy and sad as I watch my kids handle this stressful situation. They know why we are here, and that Disneyland and the beach is just a sidebar. Meaghan says she would like to go down to the beach to find the perfect location for her mom.

I think it's a little early for that, but we agree, and I instruct everyone to put their suits on so we can make it a day at the beach. With that, Meaghan volunteers to get ice for our ice chest.

"Cool," I say, and Caleb walks out with her.

Bailey tells me she is worried.

"About what, honey?" I ask.

"I think Meaghan doesn't want us to drown her mom in the water."

"Bailey, we are not drowning her. Do you understand that we are honoring Aunt Deb by spreading her ashes into the ocean?"

Bailey says, "Never mind," and leaves the area so she can retrieve her beach toys. With that, she is done talking about it.

We spent the day playing in the sun. Everyone helped bury Caleb in the sand. At one point, the only thing that makes him resemble a person is his head. Meaghan put a ball cap on it, and the people walking by did not even notice there was a person there and at times, almost tripped over him.

By afternoon, we had all been in and out of the water, running up and down the beach and throwing a ball around. How did we get so sunburned?! We used sunscreen all day. Somehow, we never looked for the "final resting place," and I assume we will revisit it tomorrow.

Ana is flying in at seven, so we need to get moving. The kids are excited to show her our room, and I am excited to see her face. I always find myself missing her. Driving to the airport at night is stressful. Caleb has a difficult time navigating, and I can tell he is a little overwhelmed, too. Maybe it's because he is in a car with all girls and there is about to be one more.

He and Ana have always been close, just like he and Meaghan, but he is still acting a little strange. From the interstate, we can see the lights of the airport, so we know we are driving in the right direction.

Once we leave the airport with Ana, everything returns to normal. We are together and where we are supposed to be. It feels right, and for the first time in a very long time, I feel at ease. I will never forget my sister, but I must get on with my life. We all do. Tomorrow is probably going to be rough on us all, so we need to laugh a little tonight. After all, that is precisely what Deb would say: "Laughter, even just a little, will make a difference in your outlook."

Later, the decision is made to go to Disneyland tomorrow. We are all dressed and ready to go, and almost to the door when Meagan tells us to hold on. She walks across the room to get Deb. She wants to bring her with us.

I ask Meaghan, "Are we taking her to Disneyland with us?"

Bailey bursts out laughing, which sort of catches us by surprise. It is funny, and it breaks the loud silence. Caleb picks his sister up and whispers something in her ear. After that, I notice she rests her hand on Meaghan's shoulder while we ride the elevator down to the lobby.

Once in the car, Deb is placed in a seatbelt between Meaghan and Ana. There is no further conversation about it — our new normal.

While driving to Disneyland, the kids are caught up in small conversations about this or that. They are excited, and each one wants to do something different once inside the park. Bailey, of course, wants to meet all the princesses, which will take time. Caleb thinks it is lame and wants to go on the "big" rides. Meaghan and Ana are quiet.

I believe they are experiencing guilt, the ugly monster that rears its head most unexpectedly. I know it personally. I want them to have fun, and I know Deb would want that, too.

However, I understand that feeling of guilt. How can I help them deal with this and show them it is okay to have fun? It is Ana that brings Meaghan around. She is laughing and telling stories about the last time we had all been together before Deb was diagnosed.

"Do you remember when Mom and Tia were on the Ferris wheel, and they were in the car above us? It was funny because Mom was scared, and Tia made it worse for her by rocking the chair."

Meaghan found that story calming as she remembers her mom's laughter. It's the first glimpse of a smile today. Score Ana! By the time we are in line to buy our tickets, they are chatting it up about what they will do first. After 12 long hours, we leave the park at midnight.

Everyone is hungry again, so we make a run for fast food. Ana's flight back to Albuquerque is at 8:00 p.m. tomorrow, so we will need to spread the ashes early in the day. It officially feels like we might "really" be on vacation.

I am awakened in the morning by the kids goofing around on the balcony. This is Ana's first trip to California, and she is in love with the ocean. Meaghan made coffee for us, and I have a hot cup waiting for me. While standing out on the balcony, all I see, and feel is love. The thought of spreading Deb's ashes is not at the forefront of our minds. Instead, and in its place, is the hope of a good life.

Ana and Meaghan are making plans to come back to California in a few months, and Caleb thinks he will move here after college. The kids want to spend time on the beach, so they already have their suits on. I put mine on, too, and we leave the room without Deb this time.

Our time is limited, and in the interest of saving time, the kids decide to hang out on the beach close to the hotel. Caleb is already sunburned, so he is playing it safe by wearing a t-shirt and baseball cap.

Bailey is running around half-naked because her suit is a little snug. I notice the scar on her hip, where they removed the melanoma — a clear reminder of hope. I hope for a new future for us all. To our surprise, when Ana takes off her t-shirt, she has the same swimsuit on as Meaghan. I hear them talking about it, too. They are surprised because they were not together when they bought them. True sisters! A little later, Bailey and I head up to our room to shower while the teenagers continue to hang out on the beach for another hour or so.

By the time they got up to the room, Bailey and I were done getting ready. The girls are quick, and so is Caleb, and we plan to go to dinner after we spread the ashes. I bought the kids new clothes for this, and I am wearing a beautiful pale yellow sleeveless linen dress.

I did not want to worry about shoes while walking on the

sand, so I chose clothes that would be nice for doing this. There are not many opportunities for us to dress up. Caleb looks handsome in his new outfit, and Deb would be thrilled at how nice her girls look.

It has already been a long trip, so I am glad we are getting this part over with now. Earlier, I had forgotten to call Jake for advice about the ashes, so I guess we are honestly winging it. We drove up the coast for over an hour before seeing a place where we could have privacy as well as ease of accessing the area. There are signs posted along most of the beaches that clearly state you cannot dump human remains into the ocean: "No spreading of human or animal remains is allowed in this area."

I have four other people relying on me, and we *are* going to spread her ashes! Even if it means I get fined. We finally found our spot, and Meaghan carried Deb out of the car. She is holding on very tight. It is a little bit windy but a glorious day.

I have scoured the area and have not seen another soul nearby. I also have not viewed any posted signs, so I think we are good to go. Ana is holding Bailey's hand as we walk down the hill toward the ocean. There are cliffs just up the beach, and I know Deb would have loved this view.

Once we got down to the beach area, suddenly, I feel anxious as I look into the eyes of these kids. Meaghan and Ana are both softly crying. Caleb and Bailey look startled. I did not have a speech ready, so I asked if we should say a few words, but Meaghan, Ana, and Bailey are crying. They can't speak. I am choking on the lump in my throat but know I must speak up. Now is my chance to say something meaningful — not empty words.

After a long silence, Caleb says a prayer. I do not remember the words said, but I do remember how very precious and amazing my son was on that beach. By him taking the lead, one by one, each one of us said a little something.

Again, I wish I could share with you what we each spoke, but like Caleb's prayer, all the words are lost deep in my heart – our hearts. What I can tell you is you would not be able to find more love between five people ever.

While standing there, holding hands with Deb sitting in the sand between us – we are one. We are honoring her with our presence and with our words. I am unsure about how we will ever recover from this moment. It was much harder than I ever thought it would be. As I look into the kids' eyes, I know their grief is profound. The thoughts of her last days in the hospital flood my mind, and I wish I could have been smarter then and smarter now.

Once we are finished speaking, it seems natural to begin spreading the ashes, so I take the lead. I took the lid off the vase and hand it to Meaghan and turn away to walk toward the water. The kids follow closely. I can feel them, which is a little stressful too.

There can be no mistakes. This must get done correctly. Once the ashes are gone, they are gone. No do-overs. Is there a right or wrong way to do this? I wonder. Nothing comes to mind.

While standing in a couple of inches of water, I begin to bend over to spread the ashes. Out of nowhere, a gust of wind invades our ceremony, creating the biggest mess! When I stand up and face the kids, the looks on their faces horrifies me. They are all freaked out. Even Caleb loses his cool. Unbeknownst to me, the gust of wind scattered Deb's ashes all over my face and dress. I am literally *wearing* Deb. Before we left the hotel, I had slathered extra moisturizer all over my arms, face, and neck to treat my sunburn. The ashes were now all sticking to the lotion.

Caleb blurts out, "Mom, you have Aunt Deb all over your face."

"What?!?" I panic. Now I can taste her. Taste the ashes. They are up my nose, in my eyes and mouth — I am covered in Deb.

After Meaghan hears Caleb say this, she begins crying hysterically. But Bailey starts her contagious giggling, and this has Caleb, and I doubled over laughing, too. I am trying to joke about it, but Meaghan isn't laughing.

Startled, Anna starts laughing about it and says, "I guess we won't be going to dinner now, Tia."

It doesn't take long for Meaghan to calm down and see the humor in it. This is our life. Nothing is ever easy. It is not a perfect day, but it is an okay day: a quick and dirty memorial, Denine style. I know somewhere out there, up there, *my sister had the last laugh*.

Once again, with the vase in hand, Caleb takes charge and walks out until the water is up to his knees. He leans over and gently swishes the jar back and forth until it is empty. We join him, splashing around and enjoying the view. A sense of peace sweeps over us. We will all be okay now.

The thing about our need for laughter in this family is simple. It is like the duct tape mom used when we were little. She ran duct tape all around our bedroom window after I was almost kidnapped. We slather duct tape on everything. Duct tape is our laughter. It can mitigate a multitude of pain and anguish. We rip it off bit by bit until a fat scab is all that is left. And today, we have ripped off another strip of duct tape in hopes of quick healing.

After leaving Ana at the airport, we drove back to the hotel in total silence. One by one, the girls each fell asleep. Caleb flips through the radio channels when he stops on a song. A beautiful song. It is Elvis's song, "In the Ghetto." For the first time during this trip and while singing along, my son finally cried.

As the elevator stops at our floor, I feel butterflies in my stomach. I take it as a sign from my sister: a nudge -her approval of our day.

It could have also been the surprise of opening the door to our room and seeing my husband standing out on the balcony with a beer in his hand. We ran to him. I pulled away for a second to witness my kind husband hugging these kids tightly. I can see it. I see our future.

After a year of chaos and pain, my sister left us. To say I am smarter today might be right. To say I am a different person today, hell yes! Do I dare say aloud we are okay? As a family, we were hit where it hurts most — in our hearts. We have learned significant life lessons during this process. So yes, I do see a bright future. This family has survived to live another day. My family! My *real* family.

I am relieved my sister is no longer suffering, which is how I have been able to move on. I am excited to see where the next chapter takes us. Everyone is grieving in their own way, so my resolve is to tread lightly from now on. And not just with my family, either.

I believe every single person I know has lost someone close and is scarred by that pain. They must live their story, too. Except for Jake. He has not experienced the pain of losing a loved one. Not yet. His day will come and, luckily for him; he is a benefactor of my pain and the painful lessons the universe taught me. I am prepared to help him and, hopefully, I will know what to say to help lessen the sting, but he will need to *feel* it – experience it for his own personal growth.

From the day my sister found the tiny lump in her breast to the day she died was less than a year. I started writing this book a few years after she died 20 years ago —a true love story about how our lives changed during that short year.

Five years after Deb left this world, she appeared to me late one night in my bedroom. Sadly, that would be her last visit. We chatted about our many screw-ups and how we survived it all. Then she pushed on me to answer one question: "What in the hell are you wallowing in self-pity for?"

That night, she helped me see that I was in dire need of self-care. Like her, I loved to drink. It helped me stay numb and feel sorry for myself. With Deb's words echoing in my head, I regained control of myself and my life. I deleted the 80,000-word memoir I had written and started all over.

I've emerged, healed. I finished the cathartic second draft of 59,600 words. This version is more of a love story, absent of the bitterness that flowed through my first draft. My sister Deb was an amazing and caring person. She was an alcoholic, hippie, and the *love of my life*.

After her death, I felt the worst crippling sadness I had ever felt in my entire life, and **empathy** was the last lesson she taught me, just two months before she died. I often wonder what she would look like today.

During the first few months immediately after her death, she visited me more regularly. She visited me at night and in my bedroom. To me, she was real. She would sit at the end of the bed, talking to me. I would awaken to the sounds of her scratchy voice. Each time it sounded like she was thirsty, or that she had just awoken herself and needed to clear her throat.

"What are you doing with your life, Denine? Are you happy? Do you think I was a good mom?"

The conversations were one-sided. I lay there in awe of her visits. **She came back to me**. Over the years, I have learned to parlay my grief into something else: work, kids, marriage, and this book. I feel strongly about many things. I fight to be clear about my beliefs, too. You will never find me "sitting on the fence." Although I may not be a leader, I am definitely not a follower!

After all of this; all of the failures in my life, I get it. I understand what the universe had to teach me. Gratitude is only found in the present. To that extent, I am grateful for my life lessons. It brought me to where I am today and my life is good. Thank you universe for all you have taught me. I am eternally grateful.

Any crime against children makes me sick, and I am very outspoken about it. We live in a culture where it seems to me what used to be good is now bad, and vice versa. I do not understand this. I cannot help but wonder what I would have missed had I been raised by that other family that I was given to shortly after my birth. Or worse yet, had the creep that tried to kidnap me when I was only seven - raped, tortured, or killed me. I would have missed all of it. Everything! Sadly, it took me a very long time to recognize my good fortune and feel gratitude.

The lessons learned by being in love with my sister taught

me a lot about life. Today, I feel absent of regrets. My life has turned out pretty good. I am generally a happy person and am proud of my life as a mom, wife, grandma, and friend to many.

Grief from the loss of a sibling takes you on a journey that, in my opinion, few survive. Other than your parents, a sibling is your closest relationship in life. And it's always the easiest to forgive.

THE END

Made in the USA
Las Vegas, NV
07 September 2021